22 DAYS IN ALASKA

THE ITINERARY PLANNER

BY PAMELA LANIER

Other Books by Pamela Lanier
Complete Guide to Bed & Breakfasts, Inns and Guesthouses in the United States and Canada
The Bed & Breakfast Cookbook
Elegant Small Hotels
The All-Suite Hotel Guide

This book is dedicated to protecting the environment and saving the great whales.

Special thanks to Bill Marchese, Keith Fernandez, Gordon Thorne, Beverly Phillips, Kathy Moore, Becky Paul, Gert Seekins, Sue Lyon, Rick McIntyre, Nancy Medlin, Tom Griffiths, Lee Hamme, Sue Hankinson, Judy Countryman, Kent Williamson, Linda Holmes, Doug Barton and Robert Butterfield.

Library of Congress Catalog No. 87-043134

Published by
John Muir Publications
Santa Fe, New Mexico
Printed in the U.S.A.

Editor   Richard Harris
Design/Production   Mary Shapiro
Maps   Janice St. Marie
Cover Map   Tim Clark
Word Processing   Rita Guidi
Typography   Copygraphics, Inc.

ISBN 0-912528-68-0

CONTENTS

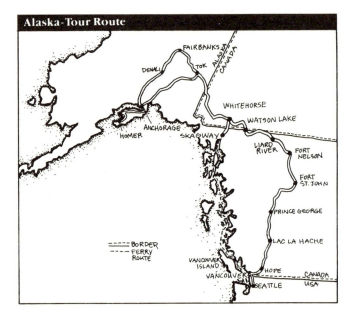

Alaska-Tour Route

FAIRBANKS

TOK

DENALI

ALASKA

CANADA

WHITEHORSE

WATSON LAKE

ANCHORAGE

HOMER

SKAGWAY

LIARD RIVER

FORT NELSON

FORT ST. JOHN

PRINCE GEORGE

LAC LA HACHE

- - - - BORDER
- - - FERRY ROUTE

VANCOUVER ISLAND

VANCOUVER

HOPE

CANADA

SEATTLE

USA

HOW TO USE THIS BOOK

Few places in the United States evoke as much curiosity and excitement as Alaska. Your Alaskan daydream may be that of an RV camper on a quest for adventure along the Alcan Highway, a nature lover in search of North America's finest wildlife viewing, a passenger admiring pristine misty islands from the deck of an Inside Passage "Blue Canoe"—or all of the above. This book will guide you on your way to making your vision of Alaska become a reality.

22 Days in Alaska takes you through some of the most stunning scenery on earth: Kluane National Park in the Yukon, bordered by the world's largest non-polar ice field; Portage Glacier, where you can walk up almost to the face; Kachemak Bay, an exquisite, teeming marine life habitat surrounded by craggy peaks; the charming artists colony of Homer; and Denali—at 20,320 feet, North America's highest peak.

The 22-day itinerary begins in Seattle, Washington, the closest city to Alaska in the lower 48 states. It takes you through the barely populated forests of British Columbia and the Yukon Territory, then on up the Alcan Highway to Anchorage, the hub of Alaska's highway system. In the next two weeks, tour the part of the state that can be reached by road and venture by boat, plane, horseback or on foot into the wilderness beyond. The majesty of Denali is a climax that's hard to beat, and then three days on a ferry or cruise ship down the Inside Passage, surely among the world's most scenic water routes, let you relax amid visual splendor before you return home.

If you have extra time, enjoy this itinerary at a more leisurely pace, dallying for as long as you like at each destination and taking advantage of the side-trips and options I've described. If you don't have 22 days, pick the part of this itinerary that appeals to you most. Denali National Park, Homer, or even Barrow at the northernmost tip of Alaska, would be great. You could buy a round-trip plane ticket to Anchorage, use this book's public transportation appendix from there, and go watch the midnight sunset.

The itinerary allows for change according to your personal interests and whims. Customize it and make it your own. Take a pencil and draw lines through some sentences, circles around others, scribble notes in the margins. As you talk with campground neighbors and B&B hosts, refine your plan further.

In this book's 22 "Days" you'll find:
1. An **Introductory Overview** for each day.
2. Hour-by-hour **Suggested Schedules** that tell how long it takes to drive the route at ordinary prevailing speeds and help organize sightseeing and activity time at each destination.

3. Lists of **Sightseeing Highlights**, rated ▲▲▲ Don't miss;
▲▲ Try hard to see; ▲ Worthwhile if you can make it.
4. Clear, easy-to-read **Maps**, as well as **Travel Route** information that a co-pilot can read aloud when you can't take your
eyes off the road.
5. **Food** and **Lodging** recommendations, for non-campers
and those who wish to pamper themselves before hitting the
road again, including a selection of outstanding bed-and-
breakfasts (B&Bs) where you can spend an evening "at home"
with genuine Alaskans.
6. **Itinerary Options** for those who have more time.
   In addition, you'll find insights, information and helpful hints
to enhance your trip in the appendix and strategically located
throughout the book.

How Much Will It Cost?
This is a trip for the adventurous of all ages and pocketbooks.
Depending upon how you choose to do it, you can rough it or
travel in luxury all the way.
   Although Alaska has a reputation for being very expensive, I
assure you it need not be. This drive/boat itinerary is based on a
moderate budget, beginning at approximately $2,000 for a cou-
ple carefully watching their budget. $3,000 for a couple would
allow for more activities and for more eating out.
   Estimated trip costs break down like this:
   Gas, at 15 miles per gallon, and approximately 4,500 driving
miles, will cost $300 (allow more if your rig is big), plus $100
for oil and miscellaneous.
   Food, cooked at your campsite, will cost about $10 per day
for two people; or, eating out at moderately priced restaurants,
$50 per day.
   Lodging: Camping fees average $5 per night per vehicle;
Hostels average $6 per night per person; Hotels or Bed &
Breakfasts will run $35 and up per couple.
   Ferry tickets southbound on the Inside Passage will cost
about $200 per person for passage, plus $168-191 for a 2-person
cabin, and $575 for an average van.
   Most tourist attractions mentioned in this book are either free
admission, inexpensive, or nature's own splendor.
   On a budget, in a vehicle, plan on camping and cooking in.
Accommodations and meals are what really add up.
   It is possible to return south by road, rather than on a ferry
through the Inside Passage, thereby saving a considerable
amount of money, though you would miss one of the most
breaktaking cruises anywhere.

Because prices change so quickly, I have arranged food and lodging in price categories. They are:

Lodging (for an average double)
    Budget = under $30
    Moderate = $30-$60
    Luxury = over $60
All camping falls into the budget category, with one night's campsite (no hookups) rarely costing more than $10.

Food (full dinner per person, no drinks)
    Budget = up to $8
    Moderate = $8-$16
    Expensive = over $16

Car and RV Rental
Car rental in Alaska is comparable but slightly higher-priced than in the lower 48. The price for a compact ranges from $21 to $52 daily, and that includes 100 to 150 free miles. Weekly costs for a compact range from $130 to $364 and includes 700 to 1,000 free miles.

Avis offers one-way rentals in the state. This means that you could pick up a car in Anchorage and drop it off in Skagway if you were following our itinerary. Telephone numbers for the car rentals are: Avis-800-331-1212, Anchorage number is area code 907-243-4300; National-800-CAR-RENT, Anchorage number is area code 907-274-3695; Rent a Wreck-907-561-2218.

It's possible to rent an RV in Alaska. A mini-camper that sleeps up to 5 runs from $115 to $140 per day, plus 15 to 20 additional cents per mile. Weekly rates can bring that price down to about $100-125 per day, plus mileage. Insurance coverage is additional. Contact Murphy's RV Rental in Anchorage at 907-276-0688, or Number One Motor Home Rental at 907-277-7575. At this time, it is not economically feasible to rent an RV to drive from Seattle to Anchorage due to very high per-mile costs.

Entering Canada
American citizens can enter Canada without difficulty. You need a driver's license, voter registration, birth certificate, or passport. Naturalized American citizens should bring their naturalization papers. Travelers from other countries should check with the Canadian Consul or Embassy regarding entry requirements.

You may be asked to show sufficient funds to get you through
Canada. At least $200 US cash is advised. Credit cards may also
impress officialdom if cash is lacking.

Taking a Vehicle into Canada

Motor vehicle entry into Canada is usually quick and routine.
You'll need to show your vehicle registration. A Canadian
Inter Province Motor Vehicle Liability Insurance card is also re-
quired. You can only get one from your insurance agent in the
United States, so be sure to see him for one before you leave.
U.S. driver's licenses and those of other countries are valid
in Canada.

Driving

Most of the Alcan is now hard-surfaced, but there are still some
extensive patches of gravel. When driving on a gravel road, be
very cautious. It is possible to "spin out," particularly on a steep
grade, of which there are several on this trip. Be careful not to
drive too fast even on the smooth paved parts of the road. Right
in the middle of a 55-mph stretch you might encounter one of
Alaska's legendary 5-foot potholes. Canadian drivers do drive
fast. You don't have to follow their example. I recommend staying well within the speed limit, which in Canada is 50 mph and
in Alaska, 55 mph.

Individual driving styles differ. Some people prefer to take a
mid-day siesta and drive on into the evening. It doesn't get dark
at night until 9:00 pm in August, or 11:00 pm in June, so it's
possible to put in evening driving hours. I do not recommend
that you drive after dark in Canada or in Alaska. There are too
many animals on the road, and too many uncertain road conditions. Drive with your lights on at all times on the Alcan.

If some driving days are too long for you, stop early, and then
the next morning get an extra early start. All along this road is
an incredible assortment of camping sites, provincial parks,
commercial camping areas, and small towns with motels and
hotels. If you need to stop, do! If, however, you are in a burning
hurry to get there, and have two drivers, the whole trip can be
speeded up by one day (Seattle to Anchorage in five days instead of six).

If you think you are lost, you probably are. Don't hesitate to
stop and ask.

Maps and Road Names

You will need a good road map. American Automobile Associa-
tion members can get an excellent map and Triptik free. The
Rand McNally maps are also good, as is the map that comes in
The Milepost travel guide.

Alaskans like to call their highways by names rather than by numbers, which is colorful but can be confusing. The names of Alaskan/Canadian highways you will be driving on this trip, by name, highway number and destination, are:

Alaska Highway (aka The Alcan)—Dawson Creek, British Columbia to Fairbanks, Alaska. In British Columbia, Route 97. In the Yukon, it becomes Highway 1. At the Alaskan border it becomes Highway 2 to Fairbanks.

George Parks Highway—near Anchorage, to Fairbanks, Highway 3.

Glenn Highway/Tok Cutoff—Highway 1, Tok to Homer.

Klondike Highway—Skagway, Alaska to Alaska Highway near Whitehorse, Highway 2.

Seward Highway—Anchorage to Seward, Alaska Highway 1 at Junction, becomes Highway 9.

Sterling Highway—Junction on Seward Highway to Homer Highway 1.

Camping

Tent and van camping is wonderful up north, definitely your best bet for an inexpensive vacation. Tent campers will need a good quality tent with an intact mosquito net, rain fly and waterproof bottom, as well as lightweight sleeping mats and sleeping bags.

Roadside camping in Canada is readily accessible. The road through British Columbia and the Yukon has many pull-offs and a large number of provincial parks, almost all of which have camping facilities. Campsites tend to be basic, with a fireplace, picnic table, outhouses and water. The cost for Canadian provincial parks is $5 overnight ($25 per season)—that is, if the ranger gets around to collecting it. They are understaffed.

In Alaska, campsites abound on state, national and provincial park sites, commercial sites, or just off in the bush. Alaska state law does not prohibit camping by the side of the road.

Other possibilities for roadside camping are the many turnouts, rest areas marked by rectangular blue signs, and scenic viewpoints. All these can make good campsites. The rest areas sometimes have signs saying, ''No overnight camping allowed,'' but I've never met anyone who has been rousted from one.

If you find yourself tired in an area where you don't see a pull-out, or feel timid about using one, pull into one of the gas stations which are located no more than 50 miles apart all along the Alcan. Get a fill-up and ask if you can stay overnight in their parking lot.

Never bring food into your tent. When in bear country, pack all food inside your vehicle. Don't leave even crumbs outside, or you can expect unwelcome and potentially dangerous late-night visitors. If you are backpacking, put food in a covered container a good distance from your tent.

Mosquitos

Mosquitos are more than a nuisance in the summer in the north country; they are a genuine problem. Be vigilant. Keep your windows rolled up and the vehicle closed when you stop. Get in and out of the vehicle quickly and close the doors, or dozens of the little devils will enter in a minute. Don't park by water for picnics or overnight, if possible. Beware of walking into the shade. Mosquitos love the shade. Buy high-test bug repellent and purchase mosquito coils, available in most general merchandise stores in Canada. Burn a coil for 20 minutes while you are out of the vehicle; that will kill the mosquitos. It doesn't smell too good, though. Don't become a mosquito dinette— wear a long-sleeved shirt and pants.

Clothing

Many people think of Alaska as a land of perpetual ice and snow, but a 90-degree July day in Fairbanks will dispel that notion. Within this enormous state's 586,000 square miles, a vast assortment of climate and geography occurs. In fact, Alaska could be spelled "Alazka," because the weather runs from A to Z. The most extreme temperatures are found inland. Coastal areas are more moderate, but damp and chilly most of the time. A lot of rain falls in southeastern Alaska and in south central sections along the coast.

The weather is highly changeable in the summer, going from overcast and chilly, to bright, sunny and hot all within the space of a few hours. The motto is, BE PREPARED FOR ANYTHING.

The guidelines for dressing in Alaska are "comfortable and casual." In general, dress as you would for the climate in the Pacific Northwest or the New England states. Always be prepared for rain. It makes the most sense to dress in layers so you can take them off or put them on as the weather changes.

A typical day's attire might start out with warm socks, tennis shoes, jeans, an undershirt or turtleneck if it's really cold, a wool sweater, your water resistant jacket and a bandana tied around your neck. If the day warms up, you can take off the jacket and the sweater. Don't forget to pack T-shirts and shorts. You could luck out and have real summer weather. You might want to pack fewer T-shirts than you will need and buy them along the way as souvenirs. A long-sleeved, lightweight shirt is de rigueur for warm summer evenings when mosquitos, the so-called Alaska state bird, are out in droves.

Pants are acceptable for women everywhere, and even in the best restaurants you will find people dressed in jeans. The style-conscious are glad to have a dress-up outfit for city nightclubs and fancy restaurants.

Comfortable shoes are a must. Tennis shoes have taken over in Alaska, although you may want specialized climbing and hiking shoes if you intend to go far off the beaten track. Rubber boots would be handy in the southeast and south central regions, but if you don't have them, make sure you have at least one change of shoes in case those you are wearing get wet. It's a rule of the north that if your head is warm and your feet are warm, the rest of you will be warm. Bring extra socks—preferably wool socks—and bring a hat. Have a bandana (a marvelously versatile item) with you at all times. A lightweight waterproof jacket which zips up the front, with a hood, will prove indispensable and easily gotten into and out of as the weather changes.

If you are going to be doing a lot of boating, then you will need a rain hat, rain jacket or parka with a hood, and rain pants.

Bring a swimsuit? Sure! Many hotels have pools, and you'll be stopping in several hot springs where bathing suits are required.

Road Food

The best way to eat well and really enjoy what you came up north for—a quiet time in the magnificent surroundings—is to picnic frequently and prepare simple campsite dinners and breakfasts.

A shopping list for a well-stocked camping pantry might include butter, oil, evaporated milk in small cans, peanut butter, jam or jelly, granola, Familia or your favorite cereal, cheese (Monterey jack or mozzarella are good all-purpose cheeses) raisins, prunes, nuts, canned chicken, sardines, spaghetti, spaghetti sauce, parmesan cheese (already grated), ramen, other packaged or canned soups, chicken bouillon cubes, spices such as fine herbs or oregano, tomato paste in a tube, mustard, a small bottle of vanilla, salt, pepper, vinegar, instant coffee, cocoa and tea (Constant Comment is a good choice because you can use one tea bag for several cups of hot water), cookies and chocolate bars.

Stock your ice chest with fresh bread, milk and vegetables every two or three days. Apples and oranges keep well, as do cucumbers, green onions and cabbages.

For quality food at the cheapest prices, shop in the U.S. or near the border in Canada. Canada is a land of ethnic and cultural diversity, and the markets there are bursting with goodies. Make a major provisioning stop in British Columbia's densely populated corridor area at the shopping mall in Chilliwac. Most of the brand name items you know and love are there, as well as delightful local foodstuffs like fine Canadian honey and a vast assortment of good sausages. Most large stores have in-house bakeries that turn out good bread. Great cookies and chocolate bars are a national passion.

Shop for enough food, except bread and milk, to last a week. Then, in Anchorage, go shopping again for another week's supply. Alaskan goodies include berry jams, smoked salmon (especially "squaw candy"), fresh berries and reindeer sausages. Also note places along the way to pick up special products like cinnamon rolls and freshly-baked bread.

In the back country, as a general rule food prices are high while quality and selection are poor.

Shop in Fairbanks or Whitehorse for the return trip. Pack a giant picnic hamper—food on the Alaskan ferry is expensive.

It helps to plan meals in advance, emphasizing ease of preparation and clean-up, without sacrificing nutrition or good taste. Bon appetit!

22-Day Cooking Gear

The most basic cooking situation for a van or a car and with two adults would be a one-burner stove. Bluet, which takes readily available propane cartridges, is small and very easy to use; pack a spare cartridge or two. A two-burner Coleman stove is also a good choice.

Take along two stainless steel pots: a small one to boil water for tea or coffee, and a medium size, holding about 2 quarts. You'll also want a small stainless steel frying pan for eggs, grilled cheese sandwiches and the like, a large metal serving spoon, a good knife, a vegetable parer, a cutting board, a stainless steel vegetable steamer insert to double as a colander, a medium-large shallow, metal bowl that can serve as a dish basin, tossed salad bowl or corn-on-the-cob cooker, a big soup bowl for each person, silverware, extra spoons, plates (ceramic, plastic or paper), ceramic mugs, glasses and a large tumbler for cold drinks. You'll want a box to keep all this equipment in one place, and another box for food.

If any piece of advice about Alaskan travel bears repeating, it's this: *never* leave food outside your vehicle in the north country. Bear bait.

Bed and Breakfast
In the past few years the bed-and-breakfast (B&B) movement has mushroomed in the U.S., nowhere more so than in the Northwest. Staying in Alaskan B&Bs provides a unique opportunity to get to know the north and its people firsthand, and I highly recommend it.

I've listed my favorite Alaskan B&Bs along this route in the main itinerary. In case you decide to venture off the beaten path, in the back of this book you'll find a list of noteworthy B&Bs situated in other parts of Alaska. For updated information and more B&Bs in both Canada and Alaska, please consult the most recent edition of my *Complete Guide to Bed & Breakfasts, Inns and Guesthouses in the United States and Canada*, available from John Muir Publications.

ITINERARY

Pleasure traveling in Alaska is best done from June 1 to
September 1 (You could leave May 15, but be prepared for some
chilly times.)

This recommended itinerary is the result of eight trips to
Alaska. It provides a very broad overview of the north country
in all its glory and the opportunity to pursue your own individual interests in selected areas whose recreational and
cultural facilities are outstanding.

It is important, when you plan your trip, that you make reservations for your return on the ferry or cruise ship; then, work
the 22-day trip around your departure date southbound from
Skagway. Following the 22-Day itinerary is a 14-Day trip
itinerary by public transportation for those with less time.

This itinerary is not written in stone, and, as a matter of fact,
contains many side trips, optional trips and post-tour choices.
Feel free to move around, and by all means, make the trip your
own, changing the schedule to suit your fancy.

DAY 1 North to Alaska. Drive from Seattle and cross the border
into Canada. After shopping in the Chilliwac area and having a
picnic lunch and dip in the lake at Hope, you continue through
the spectacular Fraser River Valley and spend the night at lovely
Lac La Hache.

DAY 2 This is a 500-mile driving day from Lac La Hache, British
Columbia, across the Continental Divide and then along the
beautiful Peace River. At Fort St. John, spend the night and connect with the Alcan.

DAY 3 Another 500-mile drive from Fort St. John is broken up
by a long afternoon stop at lovely Liard River Hot Springs. Take
time to swim, relax, clean up and make dinner before pushing
on to Watson Lake.

DAY 4 This is a short (268-mile) driving day from Watson Lake
to Whitehorse, Yukon. Arrive in Whitehorse by 2:00 pm and
take the rest of the afternoon to explore this thriving frontier
city; spend the night in town or drive a few miles out of town to
Takhini Hot Springs and camping area.

DAY 5 Today's route from Whitehorse to Tok, Alaska, winds
through an area of impressive mountains and mysterious Lake
Kluane National Park. Picnic lunch at Kluane Lake and visit the
museum of natural history. Cross the border in the late afternoon and arrive at Tok in time for dinner.

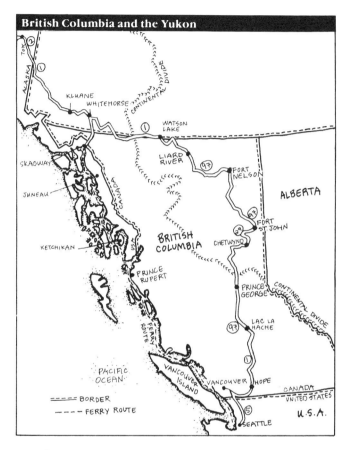

British Columbia and the Yukon

DAY 6 Tok, Alaska, to Anchorage. Today, make a classic Alaskan drive, seeing some fantastic views of mountains, lakes and Matanuska Glacier, arriving at Anchorage at 4:00 pm, with the evening free for exploration. We return to Anchorage for a full day, Day 12.

DAY 7 Today, drive a leisurely 225 miles southwest from Anchorage to Homer. The route along Turnagain Arm and down the Kenai peninsula offers fabulous scenery at every turn. Arrive at Homer at 3:00 pm, and make reservations and preparations for the next three days' activities in the area. Evening free.

DAY 8 Spend the morning on a walking tour of Homer, visit the Pratt Museum, pick up lunch, then head out East End road for a hike down the trail to Swift Creek at the back of the bay. The hike offers some of the most incredible views of the entire trip. Return to town for a free evening.

DAY 8 Alternative Or, if you prefer, spend the day touring the famous Homer Spit in the morning and then board the *Danny J* for a tour of Kachemak Bay and a late lunch at Halibut Cove, returning at about 6:00 pm. You may want to spend an optional night at Halibut Cove, returning to Homer the next day.

DAY 9 Homer is the center for world-class halibut fishing. Today you will try your luck on the high seas, leaving Homer at 6:30 am, and return about 6:00-8:00 pm, for a bite of dinner on the Spit. Then back into town for a hot tub to warm up.

DAY 9 Alternative If fishing isn't your cup of tea, take the 11:00 am boat to the historic town of Seldovia, located across the bay from Homer. The trip to Seldovia takes 2 hours through Eldred Passage, then past the shores of Kachemak Bay State Marine Park. This is one of the best trips ever for spotting wildlife in the air, on the land, and in the sea. Return to Homer in the late afternoon or spend an optional overnight in Seldovia.

DAY 10 Today you will spend the day across from Homer at China Poot Bay, hiking with a trained naturalist of the China Poot Bay society. On the way over the boat lingers at Gull Island, a fascinating bird sanctuary. Return to Homer in time for dinner.

DAY 10 Alternative Or go horseback riding along the beach towards the back of the bay, leaving Kachemak Seaside Farm on Morgan horses, riding up the beach in accordance with the tide, stopping along the way to collect shells and driftwood, pick berries, or to photograph the fabulous scenery.

DAY 11 Today you leave Homer and slowly retrace your steps to Anchorage, with a stop along the way at Stariski to view the incomparable Alaska Range at Portage Glacier Begich-Boggs visitors center and an early dinner in the lovely Girdwood-Alyeska area. Camp for the night at Bird Creek, just outside of Anchorage.

DAY 12 Rise and shine early for your day in Anchorage. Spend the day sightseeing and re-supplying for the trip onward to Denali and Fairbanks.

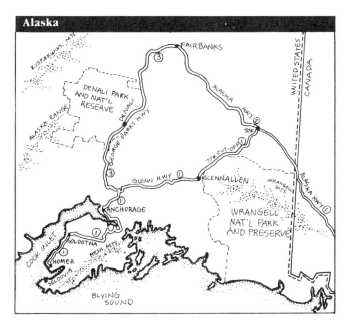

DAY 13 Northward again from Anchorage 238 miles to Denali National Park with a midday stop at the charming town of Talkeetna, arriving at Denali mid afternoon to secure reservations for your stay in the Mt. McKinley area.

DAY 14 Riley visitors center to Wonder Lake and back, 85 miles each way. This trip takes all day. This is it—your chance to view some incredible wildlife and Denali, the High One, shining in all its splendor.

DAY 15 Denali is special and this is a once-in-a-lifetime opportunity to experience a real wilderness full of life and challenge. I recommend that you spend the day hiking in the national park or, if hiking is not your thing, take a raft trip, or go flight-seeing.

DAY 15 Alternative Head back early on Day 14 from the bus trip through Denali National Park and make the 3-hour drive to Fairbanks. This alternative is ambitious—a one-day trip by plane to Barrow, the top of the world. If you want to make this trip, it is essential that you make your reservation in Anchorage. The one-day trip to Barrow departs Fairbanks mid-morning and returns early evening.

DAY 16 Today you leave Denali early for the 3-hour trip to Fairbanks. Spend the afternoon touring downtown with a must-see in the Geiss Museum at the University of Alaska campus. Spend the evening at Alaskaland or Cripple Creek for dinner and a vaudeville show. After all this wilderness, how about a little nightlife? Go out and visit some clubs.

DAY 17 Fairbanks to Kluane Lake. Spend a free morning finishing up your sightseeing. 12 noon, it's goodbye to the North and southward bound once more. After Tok, you will be retracing your steps to Kluane Lake where you will spend the night.

DAY 18 Kluane to Skagway. Today you travel 365 miles to Skagway, which may be the most beautiful drive in the north. Arrive in Skagway in time to catch your evening ferry down the Inside Passage, or spend the night.

DAY 19 Board in Skagway for the cruise south. You will board ship in the morning. The ship stops an hour later at Haines for approximately 1½ hours, and in the late afternoon in Juneau.

DAY 20 Cruise through one of the most spectacular parts of the Inside Passage. The ship stops briefly at Scandinavian accented Petersburg, at Wangell and at Ketchikan.

DAY 21 Sailing the lower Inside Passage. No stops, but plenty of scenery all around. Look for passing pods of whales and for bald eagles circling overhead.

DAY 22 Arrive in Seattle in the morning, spend the last day of your trip exploring this fascinating northwest city, and contemplating your just completed 22-day itinerary.

Joining the Itinerary from Other Parts of the U.S.
Seattle is the logical point from which to start this trip because it is also the terminus of the ferry. However, travelers coming from other areas will connect with the route in Dawson Creek.

From the Rocky Mountain States, the best route begins in Great Falls, Montana, I-5 (US Highway 91) to Dawson Creek via Calgary and Edmonton, Canadian Highways 43, 34, and 2, Provincial Highways 4, 2, 43 and 34, to connect with our itinerary on Day 2.

For people coming from areas farther east, I recommend, as an alternative to driving through the States, taking the Trans-Canadian Highway which parallels—slightly to the north—the border of the U.S. and goes through the lovely Canadian Rockies. If you do this, you will find the Trans-Canadian Highway connecting with the Rocky Mountain route in Calgary, Highway 2.

WELCOME TO ALASKA

Alaska is 1/5 the size of the Continental U.S. Not only is Alaska the largest state, if it were divided in half, it would still rank one and two, with Texas coming in number 3. From its farthest point east to its farthest west, Alaska covers almost 2400 miles, a distance greater than that from San Francisco to New York, and spans four time zones. The north-to-south distance is nearly 1400 miles. The land area of Alaska is 586,000 square miles; that's over 375 million acres. Of this, less than 250,000 acres (about 6/10 of one percent) have been utilized or inhabited by mankind.

Over half of Alaska's land area is seismically active. Ten per-cent of the earth's earthquakes occur here. The Good Friday earthquake in 1964 swallowed whole office buildings, while the tidal wave inundated the town of Valdez. Kodiak and Seward lost 32 feet of coastline. The earth's crust is further subjected to glaciation and permafrost.

Alaskan geography is wildly varied, from sand dunes above the arctic circle, to dense, incredibly lush forests, backed by 1000-foot-high sheer cliffs in Tracy Arm.

Three mountain systems delineate Alaska's land mass: the Coast Range, which includes the Kenai, Chugach, Kodiak and St. Elias ranges; the Alaska/Aleutian Range; and the Brooks range. There are 19 mountains higher than 14,000 feet, topping out with Mt. McKinley at 20,320 feet. From that height to the offshore Aleutian Trench, 25,000 feet below sea level, is a ver-tical variation of more than 45,000 feet.

The tidal shoreline of Alaska is almost 45,000 square miles. The tidal variation in Kachemak Bay of almost 30 feet is among the world's greatest. Alaska's coastline, 33,000 miles, is longer than that of all the lower 48 states combined. The Aleutian island chain extends over 1,000 miles. Little Diomede Island, USA, and Big Diomede, USSR, are only 2½ miles apart.

Alaska has three million lakes which are over two acres in size each. This fantastic quantity of fresh water, much of it shallow, helps to explain the superabundance of mosquitos. Lake Illiamna is Alaska's largest, covering an area of about 1,000 square miles.

The Yukon River, third longest in the U.S., flows 1,800 miles. 1,400 of those are in Alaska, the remainder in the Yukon.

Fort Yukon, Alaska, recorded Alaska's highest temperature, 100 degrees fahrenheit, and also the lowest, minus 80 degrees fahrenheit. Rainfall ranges from 2 inches annually in parts of the arctic, to 300 inches annually in certain areas of the southeast.

Alaska's state tree is the Sitka spruce. The largest forest in the U.S. is Tongass National Forest near Ketchikan, with 16 mil-lion acres.

Alaska's state bird is the ptarmigan. Three-hundred-ninety-seven species of birds visit Alaska. One-hundred-ninety-seven species are year-round residents.

In the Matanuska Valley near Anchorage, a combination of rich soil and long sunlight produces 4-foot-long cucumbers and cabbages weighing over 25 pounds.

The 780 mile-long pipeline from the North Slope oilfield to the port of Valdez was the most expensive construction project ever undertaken by private industry.

More than half the world's glaciers are in Alaska—there are over 5000 of them. The Malaspina Glacier, Alaska's largest, is bigger than the State of Rhode Island. Alaska's glaciers, covering 30,000 square miles, were formed 10,000 years ago, in the Pleistocene Age, when much of Alaska was covered with ice. Valley glaciers, often described as rivers of ice, are the most prevalent type in Alaska; however, there are also rare tidewater glaciers which terminate in the ocean. The Yukon's Kluane National Park has the largest non-polar ice field in the world. Glaciers are formed and build up because, in higher elevations, tremendous amounts of snow are deposited all year. Snow builds up and compresses into ice. A glacier's compressed ice has few air bubbles and absorbs all except blue light. The brilliant blue coloration appears most vividly on cloudy days.

Yes, ice worms are real. They live between ice crystals on the surface of some glaciers. On summer evenings they come to the surface to feed on red algae and pollen grain. "Ice Worm Safaris" are conducted by forest service people on summer evenings at Portage Glacier. Go for it, then write home and tell the folks you went on a safari in Alaska.

By the way, Alaska has no snakes.

DAY 1
SEATTLE TO LAC LA HACHE

From Seattle it's an 890-mile drive to the start of the Alcan Highway on the eastern boundary of British Columbia. This leg of the trip takes two full days. Towns and tourist attractions are few, but every mile of the drive is scenic. With a full tank of gas and a clean windshield, point your rig north, psych yourself into an "on the road" state of mind, and go.

Suggested Schedule	
8:00 am	Depart from Seattle.
10:00 am	Cross the border into Canada at Alder Grove.
11:00 am	Go shopping and change money at Chilliwac.
12:30 pm	Leave Chilliwac.
1:00 pm	Picnic by the lake just north of the town of Hope.
2:00 pm	Back on the road.
7:00 pm	Arrive at Lac La Hache for dinner. Enjoy the scenic beauty. Early to bed.

Travel Route: Seattle to Lac La Hache (390 miles)
From Seattle, drive north on I-5. Just past the city of Bellingham, take Exit 256 onto Highway 539, which leads into Highway 546. This route lets you bypass the long lines of cars at the border station on the interstate and avoid the busy freeways of Vancouver, British Columbia.

Cross the border at Alder Grove. North of the border, follow the signs to Canada Highway 1. Take Highway 1 north to Cache Creek. In Cache Creek, get on Provincial Highway 297 north to Lac La Hache.

Road Highlights
The border crossing at **Alder Grove** is usually easy and friendly. Just north of the border, fruit stands selling raspberries and strawberries make for a nice snack break.

It makes sense to shop for food soon after crossing into Canada, because prices are higher the farther you get away from the heavily populated border zone. You'll also want to exchange currency and buy anything you realize by now that you have forgotten. Take the first Chilliwac exit on your right to go to the **Chilliwac Mall**, which has a bank, a Sears and several food stores. While the stores are filled with many of the same groceries you see in American supermarkets, you'll notice a few

Seattle to Lac La Hache

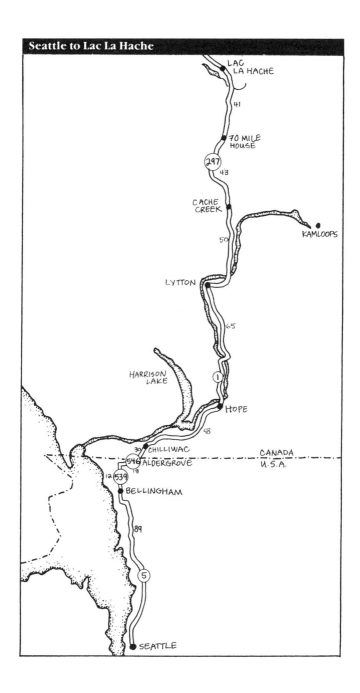

cultural differences. For example, there is an excellent selection of sausages. Perfect for traveling are the European-style chocolate-and-nut spreads and great cookies. Food shopping in Canada also presents an opportunity for a French lesson. All Canadian packages are marked in both English and French.

You will be pleasantly surprised at the bank to find that the exchange rate gives you more Canadian dollars for your American dollars. Most prices are about the same on both sides of the border, so your money will go farther in Canada.

Half an hour north of Chilliwac is the town of **Hope**. Just north of town, the divided highway ends. Immediately on your left is a lake where you can enjoy a refreshing dip and a picnic.

The afternoon portion of today's trip winds through the lovely Fraser, Quesnel and Thompson River Valleys. The town of **Litton** is western Canada's rafting capital. If you have extra time, raft trips of various durations are available. Ask in town.

Beyond **Cache Creek**, you will be on Highway 97 north. Watch out! This is a winding canyon road. The views are gorgeous; but Canadians drive fast, and road shoulders are skimpy or non-existent.

The beautiful alpine area of **100 Mile House** is a good place for the intrepid to boat, fish and swim in Lac La Hache.

Accommodations
The recommended stop for this evening, whether you want to camp or to rent a cottage, is **Fir Crest Resort**, Wool Route 1, Lac La Hache, BC Canada B0K 1T0, 604-396-7337, four miles to the north of the village of Lac La Hache. This is the kind of comfortable, homey resort you dream of. Swim if you dare. It's cold! Both campsites and basic, clean cottages are budget-priced. Each campsite comes complete with fire pit and grate.

In the town of Lac La Hache are ordinary motels in the moderate price range. **Missy's Place**, North Highway 97, Lac La Hache, BC Canada, 604-396-4423, right on the lakeside in Lac La Hache, serves fish and chips and full dinners at very moderate rates.

Or you can camp free at the rest area on the left, 5 kilometers north of the town of 100 Mile House, next to a small lake and an historic building.

DAY 2
LAC LA HACHE TO THE ALCAN HIGHWAY

Mention British Columbia and most people will think of
Canada's major west coast city, Vancouver, where most of the
population lives. But British Columbia is a huge province,
stretching from the Pacific to the Canadian Rockies, a
wilderness of cool evergreen forests, rugged mountains and
very few towns. Today you'll see a lot of central and eastern
British Columbia as you make the long drive from Lac La Hache
to Fort St. John, where you will join the Alcan Highway.

Suggested Schedule	
8:00 am	Get an early start.
12:00 noon	Stop for picnic lunch along the road.
8:00 pm	Arrive at Fort St. John, fill up tank, and have dinner. Spend the night in a hotel or camp in one of two provincial parks just north of town.

Travel Route: Lac La Hache to Fort St. John (444 miles)
Proceed north on Route 97. Eventually you'll reach the town of
Prince George (population 35,000, the largest in central British
Columbia), center of a booming timber industry. Beyond Prince
George, you'll cross to the eastern slope of the Continental
Divide. There aren't many tourist attractions, or even towns, on
this route, but there's more than enough mountain scenery to
make up for it. In Chetwynd, you'll go from the Pacific time
zone to the Mountain time zone and you may wish to set your
watch forward an hour. Take Highway 29 which parallels the
majestic Peace River. Route 29 dead-ends in the Alcan. At last!
    Turn right onto the Alcan and straight into Fort St. John
(population 9,000). Founded in 1806 as an Indian trading post,
the town is a center for the local oil, cattle and sheep industries.

Accommodations and Food
Just outside of Fort St. John as you turn onto the Alcan is the
Red Barn Pub at Charlie Lake, a famous Canadian pub.
    Campers will find good sites just north of Fort St. John at two
provincial parks, **Beatton Park** and **Charlie Lake Park**. If you
want to camp overnight on the roadside, there are also two rest
areas a few miles north on the Alcan, just past the Highway 29
junction.
    If you want to spend the night in a motel, I recommend the
low-priced **Northgate Motor Inn**, 10419 Alaska Rd., Fort St.

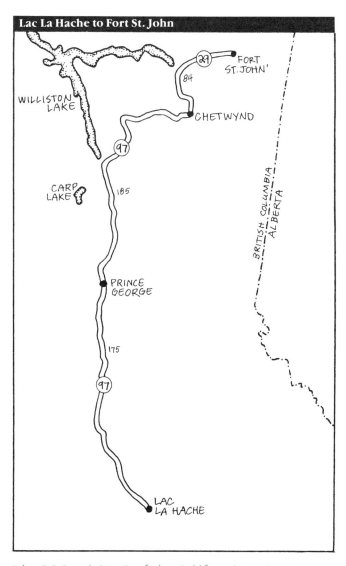

Lac La Hache to Fort St. John

John, BC Canada Z1J 1D1, 604-785-4461, right on the Alcan in the main highway services area. In front of the hotel is **Shooters Pub**, Fort St. John's nighttime hot spot.

For dinner, if you're too tired from driving to cook, try **Jade Gardens**, 1018 101st Avenue in central Fort St. John.

DAY 3

ALCAN HIGHWAY: FORT ST. JOHN TO WATSON LAKE

The Alcan Highway begins in Dawson Creek. Fort St. John is Mile 47 of the Alcan. Just 1200 more miles to Alaska! You won't make it today, but with an early start and plenty of perseverence you could reach the Yukon by nightfall. Not *too* much perseverence, though. Remember, you're on vacation, so take time to relax and enjoy Liard River Hot Springs.

Suggested Schedule

8:00 am	Breakfast and depart from Fort St. John.
12:00 noon	Picnic on the road.
3:00 pm	Arrive at Liard River Hot Springs. Spend 3 hours relaxing, swimming, cleaning up and making a campsite dinner.
6:00 pm	Push on for Watson Lake.
10:00 pm	Arrive at Watson Lake.

Travel Route: Fort St. John to Watson Lake (541 miles)
You'll spend this and the next two days on the Alcan Highway (Canada Highway 97), a legend among adventurous motorists. Built between 1942 and 1946, the Alcan opened Alaska to automobile travelers. Previously the vast Alaskan Territory had only been accessible by ferry or by rail, making it very difficult to explore once you got there.

Today you enter the great northern wilderness. Look for moose, mountain goats and birds. There is a fairly good paved road for the first 250 miles. At **Pink Mountain** (Alcan Mile 143) check your brakes in preparation for the steep grades and broken surface ahead. There is a full service lodge one-half mile before the park entrance if you need to buy anything. They also have rooms available for the truly travel-weary. **Fort Nelson** is a small town (population 1000) but the largest in this part of British Columbia. There you'll find a visitor information center and all basic tourist services. Beyond Fort Nelson there is a long gravel stretch.

Liard River Hot Springs Provincial Park (Mile 496) is a major rest stop on the Alcan. The park has campsites, hand pump water and six toilets. Park in the lot and walk over a well-built board trail half a mile to the hot springs pool. The moose that inhabit this area are frequently seen knee-deep in the warm

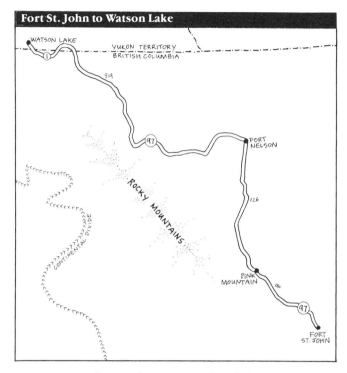

Fort St. John to Watson Lake

water, contentedly munching greens. The whole park is aglow with flowers that thrive in the warm, moist mini-climate around the springs. The springs, a large deep pool of quite hot water, are beautiful and totally natural, though surrounded by decks. A recent earthquake left the water 4 degrees hotter than it had been before.

Approaching the Yukon, you begin to enter the "land of the midnight sun," and just about everything is open late at night. In **Watson Lake**, just 12 miles into the Yukon, don't miss the famous milepost on your right. Since Alcan Highway construction workers started the tradition in 1942, town signs have been posted there by visitors from all over the world. True tourist art.

Accommodations and Food

For those who are camping, the turnoff for the **Watson Lake government campground** is 2 ½ miles west of the sign-fork, right off the Alcan, just past town. A very nice, well developed site, but beware of mosquitos.

There is a budget-priced bed-and-breakfast in town—**D&H**

Bed and Breakfast, Box 292, Watson Lake, YU Canada Y0A
1C0, Tel. 403-536-2765.

The Watson, Box 370, Watson Lake, YU Canada Y0A 1C0, a
long-time established Alcan hotel, is right in town. They have a
nice restaurant and lounge. Tel. 403-536-7781.

Also on the Alcan, just as you enter town, is the **Pizza Pantry**. They make delicious homemade bread and freshly baked
pies. If you're hungry when you arrive, by all means stop here
and buy some fresh bread to take along to your campsite.

DAY 4
ALCAN HIGHWAY: WATSON LAKE TO WHITEHORSE

The Yukon Territory, which you will traverse today and tomorrow, is a vast area of over 200,000 square miles—larger than all of New England. Yet, with a total population of only about 20,000, most of whom live in the modern capital "city" of Whitehorse, the Yukon remains a wilderness frontier that challenges the imagination.

Today's drive consists of a little less than 300 miles of generally good road and fabulous mountain scenery. Should get you to Whitehorse early in the afternoon, leaving plenty of time for sightseeing.

Suggested Schedule	
8:00 am	Breakfast and depart Watson Lake.
12:00 noon	Picnic en route.
3:00 pm	Arrive in Whitehorse. Sightseeing.

Travel Route: Watson Lake to Whitehorse (268 miles)
From Watson Lake, continue on the Alcan which, at this point, changes its designation to become Highway 1.

Whitehorse (population 15,000), the capital of the Yukon Territory, is a fascinating and colorful town. Take time to walk around downtown.

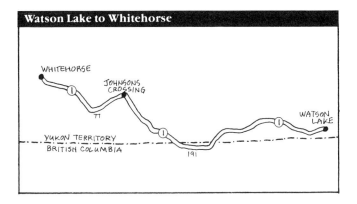

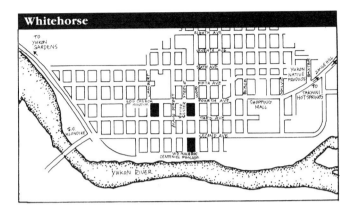

Sightseeing Highlights: Whitehorse

▲▲▲**Yukon Botanical Gardens**—The northernmost botanical gardens in the western hemisphere, they feature a spectacular display of wildflowers and a thriving vegetable garden. Watch for the botanical gardens on the left as you approach town. After visiting the gardens, go into town and park at the McBride Museum.

▲▲**McBride Museum**—This museum offers a fascinating glimpse of the territory's Wild West past. Sam Magee's cabin is on the museum grounds. In the same area as the museum, the old streets downtown have a number of colorful shops and saloons. Saunter on down to the Yukon River and view the *SS Klondike*. All 210 feet of beautifully restored sternwheeler is open to the public.

Accommodations

For campers, the best choice is **Takhini Hot Springs**. Leave Whitehorse, continuing up the Alcan, and after a few miles make a right onto the Klondike Highway (Highway 2). At kilometer 5 on the Klondike Highway, you'll see a sign directing you into Takhini Hot Springs on the left. This is a commercial establishment with a large campground and a hot springs pool. The mineral water is kept at a steady 102 degrees. There is a very clean bathhouse with unlimited hot water for showers included in the reasonable admission fee. Other facilities include a coin laundry and a nice snack bar. A laundromat is available. This is a wonderful stop for children and a good rest for everyone. Enjoy the springs, have dinner and turn in early.

There is another campground for tenters only, **Robert Service Park**, right on the outskirts of Whitehorse as you enter town.

Another idea would be to stay in one of several Whitehorse bed-and-breakfasts. Contact them for moderate B&B rates through **Yukon Bed and Breakfast**, 302 Steele St., Whitehorse, YU Canada Y1A 3Y1,, Tel. 403-633-4609. Or book your reservations directly at **Mount View Bed and Breakfast**, 58 Tamarack Drive, Whitehorse, YU Canada Y1A 4Y6, Tel. 403-633-2353. It is a cozy, country-style family home with 2 bedrooms (each with its own bath), only a few minutes from downtown Whitehorse. Complimentary tea and homemade goodies are served in the evening.

Food Shopping
It may be grocery shopping time again. Stop by **The Deli**, 203 Hanson St., for an excellent array of homemade sausages and gourmet food items from Europe. On the way out of town, the supermarket in the **Quanlin Mall** is a large, well-supplied store with its own in-house bakery. Stock up on fresh produce. Now is the time to buy food for the next 2 days' trip into Anchorage.

DAY 5

ALCAN HIGHWAY: WHITEHORSE TO TOK JUNCTION

This evening you'll finally reach the Alaskan border. The 378-mile route winds through impressive mountains, crossing back to the western side of the Continental Divide. On the way you'll see Kluane Lake and the adjoining, largely undeveloped Kluane National Park.

Suggested Schedule

8:00 am	Breakfast, and depart from Whitehorse or Takhini Hot Springs.
12:00 noon	Picnic at Kluane Lake, or stop at Burwash Landing where you can get a good lunch at the resort.
5:00 pm	Cross the border into Alaska.
7:00 pm	Arrive in Tok.

Travel Route: Whitehorse to Tok Junction (378 miles)
In the town of Champagne, keep your eyes peeled for the native cemetery with its very well-kept spirit houses. Please respect this sacred place and *do not enter*.

The highlight of this segment of the Alcan is **Kluane National Park** (pronounced "clue-WAH-nee"). The park is home to one of the continent's largest wildlife populations, including moose, caribou, Dall sheep, mountain goats, wolves, grizzly bears, wolverines and eagles. Kluane also boasts Canada's highest mountains. Mt. Logan, at 19,520 feet above sea level, is the tallest. The world's largest non-polar ice field is here, with glaciers covering more than half the area of the park year-round. Kluane's dark, jagged sawtooth peaks, protruding through the valley and glaciers, create a brooding and mysterious atmosphere.

Hint: A piece of glacial ice in your cooler will keep everything cold for days. Due to its extreme compression, the ice is *very* slow to melt.

Park headquarters, located in Haines Junction, has an excellent visual program to acquaint the visitor with the park. The park, a wilderness area with no roads and practically no trails, offers camping, hiking and backpacking. Hikers must register at park headquarters.

Fishing is prohibited within the park boundaries. However, there is excellent fishing (graylings, northern pike and sheefish)

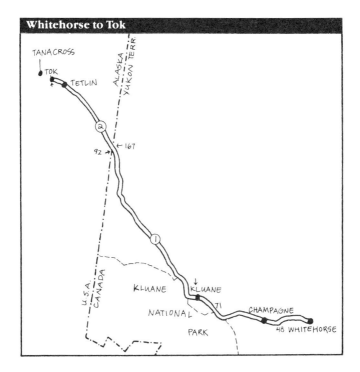

Whitehorse to Tok

across the highway in **Kluane Lake**. Stop and inquire about good fishing spots at the Visitors Center.

Kluane Museum of Natural History, at Burwash Landing, has interesting Indian artifacts, beaded ceremonial costumes, as well as all manner of creatures—stuffed.

As you near the Canadian/U.S. border, the road gets worse, and there is a patch of broken pavement. The road immediately improves at the Alaskan border.

Entering Alaska

At the border, as you cross back into the U.S., the Alcan Highway becomes known as Highway 2.

Re-entering the U.S. is easy. Have your driver's license or other ID—the same one you used to get into Canada—ready, as well as your vehicle registration. As you cross the border, which is well before the border station, notice the monument—a broad swath cut through the trees, maintained by the International Boundary Commission to mark the boundary between the U.S. and Canada.

Stop at the **Alaska Visitors Center** in Tok Junction, just before you enter town, for a free cup of coffee and lots of Alaska literature.

If you have time, visit **Tetlin** and **Tanacross**, two Athabascan Indian villages near Tok where Native American arts and crafts can be purchased. The Athabascans are best known as the ancestors of the Navajo and Apache Indians, who migrated from here to the region that is now New México and Arizona about 500 years ago. Now that you know what a long trip it is by road, imagine what it must have been like for the Indians to make the journey on foot.

Beware! Tok (pronounced "toke") is mosquito heaven. Get out the repellent.

Native Heritage
Whitehorse is the first place on this itinerary with a large population of people of Indian descent. Other areas with major Native American populations people are the environs of Anchorage, Fairbanks, Barrow and Ketchikan.

Anthropologists believe that early people emigrated to Alaska over the Bering land bridge 15,000-30,000 years ago, but there is much disagreement as to when this really happened. Some scholars believe it may have been as recently as 3,000 years ago.

Members of four ethnic groups stayed to populate Alaska: the Athabascan Eskimos (some of whom went south to become Apache and Navajo), who settled the arctic shores; the Aleuts, who populated the Bering land bridge and the Aleutian island chain; and the Tlingits and the Haida, who occupied the lush southeast.

Many of these people were nomadic, returning seasonally to favorite hunting and fishing areas. Others, especially the Tlingits and Haida, favored by a dependable food supply, only moved from summer fish camps to permanent winter residences where they evolved a complex society. All native people lived in complete harmony with their surroundings, altering the land very little. They had no written language, but passed along their history and heritage by means of dance, art, storytelling and verbal historians. At their height, there were probably 75,000 to 100,000 native people in Alaska. This number was quickly and drastically reduced by the coming of the white man with his diseases and metal-weapons aggression.

The profound difference between the native American culture and that of the Europeans is perhaps best illustrated by the fact that songs were owned by the clan, and a clan could only use another clan's songs if formally lent. The Indians held spiritual things like songs in ownership, while the land belonged to all. Or, the custom of potlatch, in which an individual's status in the community was vastly enhanced by being able to hold a huge celebration and give away valuable gifts to all of the guests.

The natives were generally a peaceable and inventive people (although the practice of slavery was very widespread among the clans). Their intelligence is confirmed by their ability to live successfully in an extremely difficult environment, one of the most inhospitable on earth. However, they were helpless against the European guns.

During the time of Russian occupation, there were no more than 600 Russians holding all of Alaska. After the U.S. acquired Alaska in 1867, no treaties were made with the native Alaskans. In 1900, the native population was estimated at 30,000. Statehood for Alaska did not settle native land claims; however, oil and the giant income it generated brought about the Alaska Native Claims Settlement Act which finally recognized the rights of Alaskan natives and gave them the economic means to enter into the mainstream of Alaskan development. Today, one of the native corporations ranks among the 500 wealthiest corporations in the U.S.

Accommodations
Campers, head straight for **Sourdough Campground**, Box 47, Tok, AK 99780, 1½ miles along the road to Anchorage—just past the junction (you will now be on Highway 1). The campground has an interesting collection of Alaskana. Tell your hostess, Rita, "Hi" for me.

Those who need a room on a super-tight budget can find it at **Tok International Youth Hostel**, Box 532, Tok, AK. In the moderate range, try **Tok Bed and Breakfast**, P.O. Box 515, Tok, AK 99780; inquire for directions at the Visitors Center.

1260 Inn, Mile 1260 AK Highway, Northway, AK 99780, Tel. 907-778-2205, is at the front door to Alaska, 38 miles from U.S. border at Northway. It's a comfy, full service country lodge with video TV and a good restaurant. Prices are moderate.

Food
If you're very hungry for dinner, enjoy an all-you-can-eat salmon bake at **Gateway Salmon Bake** on the AlCan, just before Tok Visitors Center. Or have soup and bread, a specialty at **Sourdough Campground**, very modestly priced though only served until 8:00 pm. For breakfast tomorrow morning, you can't beat the campground's sourdough pancakes with all the trimmings, served from 6:00 to 10:00 am, again very moderately priced.

DAY 6
TOK TO ANCHORAGE

On your first day in Alaska, you'll drive a distance of 320 miles to Anchorage, the hub of the Alaskan road system, where half the state's population lives. Your route will take you through fantastic scenery—lofty mountains, lakes and good views of Matanuska Glacier.

Suggested Schedule

8:00 am	Breakfast on those sourdough pancakes.
10:00 am-	
12:00 noon	Stop at one or more of the lodges along your route and soak up the pioneer spirit.
4:00 pm	Arrive in Anchorage.
Evening	Free to explore Anchorage, have dinner out, perhaps take in a show.

Travel Route
Along the road to Anchorage, Highway 1, known as the Glenn Highway, several cozy lodges serve food and sell gasoline. Stop at one or all. They are, in order of appearance:

Chistochina Lodge and Trading Post—Lots of goodies here, notably homemade pies, cinnamon rolls and especially their smoked salmon. Buy some to take along.

Gakona Lodge and Trading Post—A rustic Alaskan lodge, in the National Register of Historic Places. Their Carriage House Restaurant in the original building serves gourmet fare.

Eureka Summit—The highest point of the Glenn Highway. Here you'll get an excellent view of the Melchina Glacier, which winds through a cleft in the Chugach mountains to the south. Northwest are the high peaks of the Talkeetna Range. The Matanuska, Copper and Susitna Rivers divide here in rushing and chilling splendor.

Sheep Mountain Lodge—Stop here and look through the telescope at the surrounding mountains for glimpses of the elusive mountain sheep. This is one of the best places in Alaska to spot them. Homebaked goodies at the lodge, including huge and wonderful chocolate chip cookies. Say hello to owner David Cohen for me.

Matanuska Glacier and Valley
The final leg of our trip today takes you past the Matanuska Glacier, which comes within a few miles of the road. Then it's

on into the lush and fertile Matanuska Valley, the home of giant vegetables. The valley is also Alaska's most developed water sports area, where Anchorage residents come on weekends for fishing, sailing and water skiing. Fishermen: check out the rainbow trout-stocked Kepler-Bradley Lakes complex, four miles south of Palmer. Lakeside resorts abound. Stop at the Matanuska farm market, right on the road after you leave Palmer, and stock up on home-grown vegetables.

From there an easy drive will take you into Anchorage.

Anchorage

Anchorage is Alaska's largest city, with a population of about 250,000 including 30,000 servicemen stationed at Elmendorf Air Force Base and Fort Richardson. It's a brand-new city. In 1940 it had only 3,500 people and no paved streets. The city was rebuilt in the late '60s after the most severe earthquake in 20th century North America destroyed streets and opened cracks big enough to swallow cars and even buildings. Rebuilding happened fast as the city's population swelled during the construction of the Alaska Pipeline.

Both motorists and public transportation travelers use Anchorage as their base camp for explorations anywhere in Alaska. While Alaska is by far the largest U.S. state, its road system consists of fewer highway miles (paved or otherwise) than Connecticut, and all of them lead—eventually—to Anchorage. The city is also the headquarters of the Alaska Railroad, as well as the place to rent a car or camper or arrange a bus tour.

Anchorage is encircled by four mountain ranges—the Chugach, Kenai, Talkeetnas, and the awesome Alaska Range—which shelter it from the worst sub-arctic weather; locals refer to the area around Anchorage as Alaska's "banana belt." On a clear day you can see Mt. McKinley.

Today you'll only be passing through Anchorage, spending the night on your way to Homer. Anchorage sightseeing is detailed in Day 12.

Accommodations

In general, accommodations are expensive in the Anchorage area. This is one of the reasons we recommend only a one night stay.

Anchorage has a good selection of B&Bs:

Adam's House, 700 West 21st No. A/B, Anchorage, AK 99503-1850, Tel. 907-274-1944, moderate. This is a clean, comfortable home where the hosts take pride in providing excellent service to their guests. Transportation to their home can be arranged with advance notice.

All the Comforts of Home, 12531 Turk's Turn St., Anchorage, AK 99516, Tel. 907-345-4279, Moderate. This serene
retreat on a five-acre hillside is just 20 minutes from
downtown.

Anchorage Eagle Nest Hotel, 4110 Spenard Rd, Anchorage, AK 99503, Tel. 907-243-3433, is a luxury-priced small
hotel with kitchens equipped for cooking. Rental homes and
apartments for longer stays are also available.

Darbyshire House B&B, 528 N St., Anchorage AK 99501,
907-279-0703, moderate. You'll enjoy a spectacular view of the
inlet and mountains from downtown Anchorage. Walk to
restaurants and shops.

Grandview Gardens, 1579 Sunrise Drive, Anchorage, AK
99508, Tel. 907-277-7378, moderate. Elegant service, privacy
and a romantic environment await you in this log cabin lodge.
Choose your room from three theme suites. Relax and enjoy
the beautiful view. Transportation is available to and from the
airport.

The Green Bough, 3832 Young Street, Anchorage, AK
99508, Tel. 907-562-4636, moderate. Your host and hostess enjoy sharing their extensive knowledge of Alaska to help their
guests plan itineraries. Their large, comfortable home has a
yard, a deck and a mountain view.

Heavenly View B&B, 10740 Kasilof Boulevard, Anchorage,
AK 99516, Tel. 907-346-1130, moderate. Wake up to spectacular
panoramic views of Mt. McKinley, Cook Inlet and the Alaska
Range at this bed-and-breakfast 1600 feet above the Anchorage
bowl. The clean, comfortable rooms have king-sized beds.

The Log Home Bed & Breakfast, 2440 Sprucewood Street,
Anchorage, AK 99508, Tel. 907-276-8527, moderate. Snug
hospitality and warm Early American decor are offered in this
rugged log home located in town, convenient to shopping,
sports and transportation. Free laundry, storage and freezer
facilities.

Hatcher Pass Lodge, Box 2655, Palmer, AK 99645, Tel.
907-745-5897, low to moderate. Hatcher Pass Lodge is located
in the lovely Matanuska valley, 30 miles from Anchorage. Imagine your own private cabin, surrounded by snow capped
granite peaks, with an unobstructed 80-mile view! The lodge
has a full-service restaurant.

Other bed-and-breakfasts in Anchorage are represented by
the following reservation service organizations, whose services
are free to you; a fee is paid by the B&B. Contact: **Accommodation Alaska Style**, 3605 Arctic Boulevard, Box 173, Anchorage, AK 99503, Tel. 907-344-4006; or **Anchorage Bed
and Breakfast**, P.O. Box 110135, Anchorage, AK 99511, Tel.

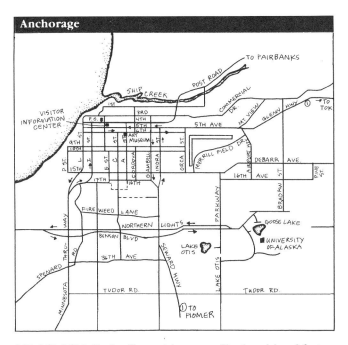

907-345-2222. Both offer a wide range of bed-and-breakfast accommodations.

For those preferring more conventional hotel accommodations, I recommend the following, all of which are centrally located downtown: **Plaza Inn Hotel**, 321 East Fifth Avenue, Anchorage, AK 99501, Tel. 907-276-7226, moderate; or **Voyager Hotel**, 501 K Street, Anchorage, AK 99501, Tel. 907-277-9501, deluxe price range. **Holiday Inn**, 239 West Fourth Avenue, Anchorage, AK 99501, Tel. 907-279-8671, is recommended for families because of the pool, sauna, laundry facilities and central location. There is a Wendy's in the building. **Captain Cook Hotel**, Fifth and K Street, Anchorage, AK 99501, Tel. 907-276-6000, can't be beat in the luxury category.

For the budget traveler, **Anchorage Youth Hostel** is located on Minnesota Drive at 32nd Avenue. It's served by People Mover and is open during usual hostel hours. Tel. 907-276-3635.

For camping, I recommend the **Centennial** and **Russian Jack Spring** campgrounds. Neither one has showers. Of the two, I prefer Russian Jack Springs.

Food

Food prices are also high in Anchorage. The least expensive food is at fast food places such as **McDonald's**, which has free refills on coffee. **Wendy's**, at the center of town on Fourth, and at other locations, has a good salad bar.

For a real Alaskan breakfast, try **Gwennies Old Alaska Restaurant**, 4333 Spenard Road, Anchorage, AK 99503, Tel. 907-243-2040, open 7 days a week. **Hogg Brothers Cafe**, 2421 Spenard Road, Tel. 907-276-9649, has great omelets, soups and croissants, and a fun atmosphere.

Chilkoot Charlie's, 2435 Spenard Road, Tel. 907-272-1010, has famous and generous free hors d'oeuvres from 4:30 to 6:30 Monday through Friday, and a free barbecue on Sundays at 6:00 pm. Kids are welcome. This is a one-stop hangout with food, a pool table, a giant TV tuned to sports events, live music, and dancing—great for mingling with Alaskans in a friendly, convivial atmosphere. Their Grande Margarita is the biggest and best in town. Free popcorn all the time.

Old Anchorage Salmon Bake, 251 K Street, Anchorage, AK 99501, Tel. 907-279-8790, serves lunch and dinner, Alaska style. This is a good place for those with a big appetite. You'll find it right downtown on the block overlooking the inlet.

If you crave Italian food (and there isn't much in the north country), **Arman Mazzi's Restaurant** at 2052 East Northern Lights Blvd., Tel. 907-279-9547, open 7 days, will be very welcome. The menu includes homemade pasta, good calzone, and my favorite, fettucini with seafood.

A drink at **The Crow's Nest Bar** atop the Captain Cook Hotel is expensive, but worth it. The view overlooks the whole of Anchorage, from the mountains to the sea. On a clear day, you can see Mt. McKinley to the north. Notice the wonderful wood floor and paneling. Opens at 5:00 pm.

Carr's Supermarket, on Northern Lights Boulevard near the intersection of Seward Highway, is the place to stock up on groceries. They also have an excellent salad and soup bar. They're open 24 hours a day. In the same shopping center are department stores such as Sears.

Nightlife

Chilkoot Charlie's, your best bet for dancing, music and partying in a convivial atmosphere, is at 2435 Spenard Road, Tel. 907-272-1010.

Alaska Experience Theatre, 705 West 6th Avenue, Anchorage, AK 99501, Tel. 907-276-3730, offers wrap-around planetarium viewing of the Alaskan landscape, animals and people at a budget price. The special earthquake room will shake you up. It's fun for everybody, but especially for kids.

Alaska Heritage Review, the Larry Beck show at the William A. Egan Civic Center, 555 West Fifth Avenue, Anchorage, AK 99501, is an excellent one-man review. It starts at 8:00 pm and the cost is reasonable.

For more entertainment, check the *Anchorage Visitors Guide*, which is free and available all over town, and the entertainment listings in the *Anchorage Times*.

DAY 7
ANCHORAGE TO HOMER

Today you'll drive 225 miles southwest from Anchorage to arrive in Homer in mid-afternoon, in time to make arrangements
for a three-day stay there. The route will take you across the
Kenai Peninsula, a major oil and gas drilling region as well as a
popular outdoor recreation area.

Suggested Schedule	
9:00 am	Depart Anchorage.
12:00 noon	Picnic lunch along the Kenai River, or other in-viting spots.
3:00 pm	Arrive in Homer. Drive directly to the end of the Spit area. Visit the tourist information cabin on the Spit and make reservations for the next three days' activities as needed.
7:00 pm	Dinner.

Travel Route: Anchorage to Homer (225 miles)
Today, we're on a straight-through itinerary to Homer. However,
when we retrace our steps in four days, the journey will be
leisurely, allowing for stops along the way.

   The drive on Highway 1, crossing the Kenai Peninsula from
Anchorage to Homer, is exquisite. Pass Mt. Alyeska Ski Resort
and Portage Glacier Recreation Area (where salmon spawning
areas can be seen), then climb over Turnagain Pass. Thirty-one
miles beyond the pass, the highway forks. Follow the left-hand
fork, which continues as Highway 1. (The other fork, to
Seward, is Highway 9.) Soon after you go through the towns of
Sterling and Soldatna into the Kenai Russian River area past the
town of Soldotna, you will catch your first glimpse of Cook
Inlet. The road follows the sea on a high bluff past Clam Gulch,
a fine clamming spot. Finally, glimpses of Kachemak Bay appear, one of the most beautiful bays in North America.

   Arrive in Homer and head straight out to the Spit. Signs point
the way through town.

Homer
Homer, nestled at the mouth of Kachemak Bay, has most of
what people visit Alaska for: spectacular views of mountains,
glaciers and fjords, and wildlife. Kachemak Bay is the richest
life-producing marine bay in North America, a resting place for
millions of migratory birds. The surrounding land is home

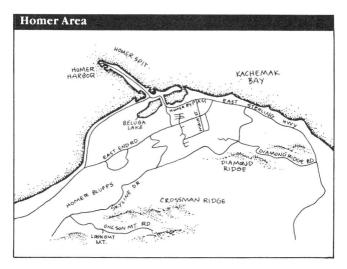

Homer Area

to moose and bears. An added attraction of the Homer area is
that there are very few mosquitos.

The Russians called Homer "Summerland" because of its
temperate climate and lush beauty. The Aleuts knew it as
"Smoking Bay" due to smoldering coal deposits. It is also
known as the Shangri-La of Alaska, because nowhere else in the
49th state do all the elements of Alaskan beauty come together
quite so felicitously.

The Spit is a unique needle of land projecting 4½ miles into
Kachemak Bay, the focal point for residents, fishermen and
tourists alike. If you're camping, find a good spot, otherwise
park near the Salty Dog Saloon and walk around. This is the
best time to make reservations for fishing trips and visits to
Seldovia, Halibut Cove or other spots. If you're anxious to fish,
try your luck off the beach in front of Land's End Resort for
Dolly Varden and halibut.

The natural gravel spit, extending 4½ miles into the mouth of
Kachemak Bay, is the second longest in the world. The Spit
sank 7 feet in the 1964 earthquake and has been washed out
several times since.

Spit denizens are known as "Spitters" or "Spit rats"! The Spit
is the lifeblood of Homer and pulses with activity all year long,
but especially in the summer.

The stunning views of Kachemak Bay and surrounding
mountains make this an ideal camping spot.

Accommodations
Camp in town at the **Homer City Campground**, Tel.

907-235-8121, at the top of Bartlett Street. Follow the signs. Facilities include rest rooms, picnic area and playground equip- ment. It's a little out of the way, but quiet, and good for families.

You can also camp on city land on Homer Spit, wherever you see other campers. A nightly camping fee is charged. There are some portable lavatories, but water is available only in a few central locations. Spit camping affords great views across Kachemak Bay, good beachcombing and some surf fishing, as well as easy access to all the Spit attractions. Camping here is somewhat noisy and busy, though. Camp super-cheap in the 24-hour area on the Spit. You have to move from day to day, and it's crowded, but usually a fee is not collected.

There is a private campground at the end of the Spit. It's more expensive but has better baths. Showers, available for an extra fee, are also open to campers using the city campground areas. Very nice public showers are also to be found at the laun- dromat on Ocean Drive. They're clean, with lots of hot water, and laundry facilities are available there too.

Camping is also available in the meadow at **Seaside Farm**.

Consider spending the night on the way back to Anchorage at **Stariski State Campground** (the campground will be on your left shortly after the town of Anchor Point). Wake up to an incomparable view of the Alaska Range.

If you want a roof over your head, many different types of ac- commodations are available. The bed and breakfasts in Homer are the best way to go. Not only do you get a nice room—and many of them are nicer than those offered by the commercial hotels—but you also get the advice of a local B&B host. The Homer B&B innkeepers are particularly enthusiastic, ready and willing to give guests the benefit of their familiarity with the area—everything from the best fishing grounds to dining recommendations.

My first choice is **Seekins Bed and Breakfast**, up scenic East Hill Road behind town, with panoramic views of Kachemak Bay and the surrounding mountains and glaciers. Gert and Floyd Seekins are your energetic hosts, who can help make your Alaskan adventure a memorable one by providing tours and charters at reasonable rates. There are lovely rooms and cabins, moderate in price, most with private baths. For in- formation or reservations, write Floyd and Gert at P.O. Box 1264, Homer, AK 99603, or phone 907-235-8996.

Other Bed and Breakfast possibilities are:

Driftwood Inn, 135 Bunnell, Homer, AK 99603, Tel. 907-235-8019. This family-owned, moderately priced ocean- front hideaway offers old-time Alaskan hospitality and breathtaking views of glaciers, mountains and Kachemak Bay. Recreational packages and family-style dining are available.

Homer Spit

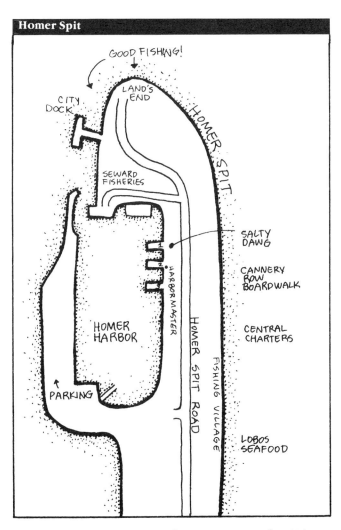

Magic Canyon Ranch, Box 632, Homer, AK 99603, Tel. 907-235-6077, moderate. Superb views of Kachemak Bay and sparkling glaciers, as well as hiking and farm fresh vegetables, are among the attractions of this comfortable ranch retreat. Your host, an Alaskan historian/anthropologist, has fascinating insights to share with you.

Quiet Place Lodge, Box 6474, Halibut Cove, AK 99603, Tel. 907-296-2212, in the luxury price range, offers peace, quiet and privacy in 4-person cabins. Excellent boating, fishing, wildlife viewing and beachcombing opportunities await right at your doorstep on beautiful Kachemak Bay. Excellent meals are served in the lodge.

Seaside Farm Cabins, out East Road, have a bed and breakfast cabin for rent, moderate, Tel. 907-235-7850. Your hostess, Mossy Davidson, has a Morgan horse farm and her own art studio on this seaside spread.

A more traditional accommodation in town is the **Heritage Hotel**, 147 East Pioneer Avenue, Homer, AK 99603, Tel. 907-235-7787, Homer's original log hotel. It has all modern facilities (yes, TV) and some atmosphere to boot.

Food

The best meals to be had in Homer are those that you prepare yourself over a wood fire out on the Spit. A fish or crab you caught, mussels and clams you collected—what a feeling!

If food foraging isn't your thing, then head on over to **Lobos Seafood** on the Spit, part way out to the boardwalk, (Tel. 907-235-5329), for perfect Homer picnic fare. They carry a wide selection of local seafood—crab, mussels, shrimp, prawns, halibut and salmon—at reasonable prices. Pick up some of their fine squaw candy (it's smoked for them the old-fashioned way, out in the country). Also out on the Spit, look for a shack selling boiled crab and shrimp plates. The prices are low and the food is usually very good.

Noteworthy restaurants in town include **Coachman's Inn** (Tel. 907-235-6565) and **Lakewood Inn** (984 Ocean Drive #1, Tel. 907-235-6144), both on Ocean Avenue on the way to the Spit. Each serves quality seafood, with prices to match.

Breakfast and lunch are bright prospects at **Hogg Brothers**, 475 Pioneer Avenue, Homer, AK 99603, serving great omelets and big sandwiches in a funky fun-filled atmosphere. The waiters are usually artists. This is a convivial spot.

Boardwalk Fish and Chips, on Cannery Row (the gray one) has good fish and chips and other things, like clam chowder. Inexpensive.

Sourdough Bakery, 1316 Ocean Drive, will be a good stop for those who love croissants and capuccino. All the pastries and other baked goods are excellent in quality. The owners even grind their own flour daily. Buy your picnic supplies here. They also pack picnic lunches for those heading out to the country.

Nightlife

Homer is a party town, with a lot of late night music, especially in the summer season. It is easy to stay up late under summer's midnight sun. For foot-stomping rock'n roll, **Alice's Champagne Palace**, right on Pioneer, is open until 5:00 am. More rock is at **Land's End Resort**, where you'll also find a great view of the bay and a full restaurant and oyster bar. Lots of dancing goes on here.

Country and western music is featured on weekends at the **Homestead Tavern**, a few miles out of town on East Road. If you're lucky, you may catch Atz Kilcher on the guitar and vocals—mighty fine stuff. Country is also featured at the **Bayside Lounge**, right on Pioneer.

You'll find jazz at the **Waterfront**, located off the bypass.

Homer Family Theatre shows movies, sometimes double features, in a fun, old-timey environment. They also have good snacks.

DAY 8
HOMER

The itinerary calls for three full days in this extraordinarily beautiful place. In the interest of diversity, I present three days' itinerary, three days' alternate itinerary, and several overnight adventure possibilities. What activities you choose depend upon your personal taste and pocketbook. Nowhere in Alaska are so many sports and adventures so readily available as in Homer. And the prices in Homer are reasonable (for Alaska).

Day 8 Suggested Schedule	
9:00 am	Breakfast in town at Hogg Brothers.
10:00 am	Make a foot tour of central Homer and visit the Pratt Museum.
12:00 Noon	Lunch in town or pack a picnic lunch to eat later along the trail.
12:30 pm	Drive out East End Road.
1:00 pm	Hike down Switchback Trail to Swift Creek.
4:00 pm	Return and drive back to town. Evening free.

Homer Shopping
Start with breakfast at **Hogg Brothers**, a great little omelet house, right in the middle of Homer on Pioneer Avenue.

Then stop next door at **Ptarmigan Arts** (471 Pioneer Avenue, Tel. 907-235-5345), which opens at 10:00 am. This is the artists' cooperative store in Homer, a great place to shop and meet some interesting locals.

Just down the street is **Toby Tyler's 8x10 Art Studio**. Toby makes a specialty of botanical paintings and prints, and he has some lovely ones, as well as a wildflower garden and herbarium with many labeled local plants.

Stop across the street at **Wild Berry Products** to taste berries and jams, and perhaps do some gift shopping. They also have early Alaskan antiques on display. If you're lucky, they'll be making jam while you're there.

Sightseeing Highlights
▲▲▲**Pratt Museum**—Located at 3779 Bartlett Street, Tel. 907-235-8635, this excellent museum of natural history has won several awards. On permanent display are artifacts from the Eskimos and other Native Americans, as well as from early pioneers; also an outstanding collection of ship models,

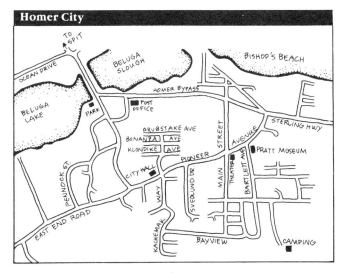

an aquarium with sea life from Kachemak Bay, and more. Open
10:00 to 5:00 daily. Small entrance fee.

▲▲**Switchback Trail**—Drive out East Road until you reach
the end which says "Bus Turnaround," approximately 16 miles.
Park there and head downhill along the trail (called East Road
extension, wide and easily discernible). Meander downward
and eventually come to Switchback Trail, which ends at Swift
Creek Beach. The two-mile hike affords fabulous vistas of
Grewingk Glacier and the Kenai Mountains. This is prime photo
country. The last leg of the trail goes by a homestead recently
settled by Russian religious refugees.

The beach near the head of the bay is great for beachcombing. Spend the rest of the afternoon enjoying the area. Berry
picking is good around here, too.

Day 8 Alternative

Tour the Homer Spit, with stops along the way, and then board
the *Danny J.* for an afternoon cruise on Kachemak Bay and late
lunch at Halibut Cove, returning at 6:00 pm.

There are lots of breakfast shop possibilities along the Spit,
including the **Hole-in-One Doughnut Shop** and, for a full
course breakfast, **Land's End**.

After breakfast, walk around the small boat harbor. The
fishermen are friendly. Crab and shrimp are for sale. You might
buy some to cook up for a Spit dinner later.

Walk farther along the Spit and take a tour of the **Seward
Fisheries**. Backtrack to Cannery Row Boardwalk and get

Day 8 Alternative	
9:00 am	Breakfast on the Spit.
10:00 am	Tour of the Spit.
12:30 pm	Get tickets for the *Danny J.* at Central Booking on Cannery Row Boardwalk (the gray one), and board at 1:00 pm.
2:30 pm	Stop in Halibut Cove and walk straight over to the Saltry for lunch.
4:00 pm	Depart Halibut Cove. Arrive back at Homer about 5.
6:00 pm	Have dinner on the Spit.
7:00 pm	Evening free in Homer. Why not check out some music?

tickets for your cruise aboard the *Danny J.* at Central Booking. The *Danny J.* departs from the small boat harbor at 1 p.m. for a scenic cruise to Halibut Cove.

For complete information on the *Danny J.*, contact **Kachemak Bay Ferry,** Box 6410, Halibut Cove, AK 99603, Tel. 907-235-7847. Or make reservations through **Halibut Cove Experience,** Tel. 907-235-8110, located at the Homer small boat harbor.

Cruise Highlights
The *Danny J.* stops at **Gull Island** to view the nine species of nesting birds there: the pelagic cormorant, the red-faced cormorant, the glaucous-winged gull, the herring gull, the common murre, the black-legged kittiwake, the pigeon guillemot, the horned puffin and the crested puffin. Large sea mammals like whales and the sea otter are also spotted sometimes on this run. Binoculars and camera equipment are a must. Rain gear might be needed too.

At about 2:30 you'll stop at **Halibut Cove**, a serene and lovely artists' community. The boat leaves you at the boardwalk which winds around Ismailof Island. There are a number of walking trails. Your tour guide aboard the *Danny J.* will point them out. I recommend that you head straight over to the **Saltry**, a really charming restaurant filled with art, at the end of the boardwalk overlooking Halibut Cove. Meals are served on beautiful, handcrafted pottery. The Saltry has an unusual and innovative menu featuring pickled fish and seafood, salmon pate, hot fish chowder, homemade bread and the best chocolate cheesecake ever. Wine and beer are also available. Prices are moderate. While on the island, visit **Diana Tillion's Art Studio** where she creates octopus ink paintings. At 4:00 pm, board the *Danny J.* for the return trip.

Check out the **Halibut Cove Experience Gallery**, an art gallery with lots of fine Alaskan art on display, located at the top of Ramp 1, Homer Harbor. Then head on over to the historic, wonderful **Salty Dog Saloon**, housed in one of the very first cabins built in this area (1897). It served as the first post office and has been a saloon since 1957. You might want to try their famous Salty Dog drink. It will take the chill off!

Overnight Option
Take the 5:00 pm ferry from Homer to Halibut Cove and spend the night at **A Quiet Place** (P.O. Box 6474, Halibut Cove, AK 99603, Tel. 907-296-2212), a charming, moderately priced lodge. Accommodations are in fully-furnished cabins. Owner Bobbie Jenkin has a canoe, a skiff and fishing gear available for guests.

Reservations may be made for the ferry through Halibut Cove Experience, Tel. 907-235-8110. The ferry returns to Homer in the early afternoon. Early morning departures are also possible sometimes.

DAY 9

HOMER

Homer is the home of world class halibut fishing. If you're a seasoned fisherman, you've no doubt already heard about it; if not, you'll find it a great place for novice fishermen to get their feet wet. Catching a big one here is pretty likely—some say almost guaranteed.

Day 9 Suggested Schedule

6:30 am	Be at the office to pay for your charter and get set. The boat leaves at 7:00. Spend all day on the high seas. Picnic lunch.
6:00-8:00 pm	Time variable. Return to Homer. Wait while your fish is fileted, then take your catch over to Katch Canning for processing.
8:00 pm	Have a bite to eat on the Spit.
9:00 pm	A hot tub at Hot Tub Emporium will warm you up.

Halibut Fishing

There are lots of charter companies in Homer, and most charge about the same (expensive) price for a long day of fishing. My favorite is **Homer Ocean Charters**, P.O. Box 2543, Homer, AK 99603, Tel. 907-235-6212, located on the gray boardwalk. Your captain, John, is one of the best on Kachemak Bay. The *Sea Witch* and *Sourdough* boats are first class, equipped with the latest fish-plotting computer. Or, go out with skipper Dan Gorham aboard the *Char-Dan*, P.O. Box 534, Homer, AK 99603, Tel. 907-235-6082. Deep Sea Charters is located on the first brown wooden boardwalk.

Homer is home to several halibut derbies, and some world records have been made here. Sign up for a derby at the boat office and be sure you have your Alaska fishing license, also available at the charter office.

Your fellow anglers aboard these trips could be from Florida or even Australia. People flock from all over the world to try their luck in Kachemak Bay. The rule here is, dress warmly. Bring rain gear and a substantial lunch. Hot water and coffee are available on board. It's always colder out on Kachemak Bay than it is in Homer. Be sure to bring a hat and gloves. The boats provide all necessary tackle and poles.

Upon your return to Homer, they will take a picture of you and your "barn-door" fish, and of everybody with a full day's catch.

Have the crew filet your catch. Then, if you get a lot—100 pounds is not unusual—take your catch over to **Katch Canning** (907-235-6241), located just up the Spit by the harbormaster's office. Velma will freeze or smoke your fish, pack it up and ship it where and when you want. Halibut jerky can't be beat. While you're at Velma's, pick up some salmon "squaw candy" or halibut jerky for picnics. It also makes a great gift!

Have a quick bite to eat on the Spit and head into town for a warm-up in a hot tub at the Hot Tub Emporium, located right behind the **Heritage Hotel** on Pioneer Avenue, Tel. 907-235-6950.

Day 9 Alternative	
9:00 am	Breakfast and a leisurely morning. Have breakfast at the Sourdough Bakery on Ocean Avenue. Then drive out the Spit to catch Rainbow Tours ship, the *Sizzler*, for Seldovia. Ship departs at 11:00.
10:30 am	Rainbow Tours office to pay for your ticket.
11:00 am	Depart from Homer small boat harbor to Seldovia.
1:30 pm	Picnic lunch or get a bite at a Seldovia restaurant.
2:30 pm	Depart Seldovia.
4:00 pm	Return to Homer. Remainder of afternoon and evening free.

Day 9 Alternative

Take **Rainbow Tours** ship, the *Sizzler*, with skipper Lee Glenden, to historic Seldovia, located across Kachemak Bay from Homer, closer to the mouth of the bay. Check in at the Rainbow Tours office on Cannery Row Boardwalk half an hour before departure. The ship leaves at 11:00 am. The price is moderate.

Note: The State ferry departs once a week, on Wednesday, at 11:45 a.m., and stops for 3 hours in Seldovia. Adults, round trip: $20; children half-price.

Skipper Lee has developed quite a reputation among bird watchers and wildlife spotters. The two-hour trip from Homer to Seldovia via the scenic route through Eldred Passage behind Yukon Island, with Sadie Peak rising majestically on the

mainland, passes by Sadie Cove, Tutka Bay, and the shores of
Kachemak Bay State Marine Park.

On one trip, some 30 species of birds were spotted, as well as
an orca whale, a minke whale, two sea otters and a bald eagle.
While you can't expect such sensational sightings every day,
Skipper Lee, who narrates the trip, seems to have an uncanny
ability to be in the right place at the right time to see wildlife.

One-and-a-half hours of free time is scheduled in Seldovia
for sightseeing. Seldovia is a small fishing village with the motto,
"city of secluded charm." Once a thriving principal seaport,
Seldovia retains most of the appearance of times gone by, in a
seaside setting ringed by mountains. A short saunter in any
direction from town will bring you to fine fishing, photograph-
ing and hiking spots. Pack a picnic lunch for Seldovia or stop by
the **Centurion Restaurant**, facing the boat harbor, moderate
to expensive. The **Kachemak Kafe** on Main Street is inexpensive for a quick bite to eat. If you like to fish, bring your rod.
The fishing is excellent from all the beaches for Dolly Varden
and humpies. Fish off the breakwater (with heavy tackle!) for
halibut.

If fishing isn't your sport, how about hiking the short trail
from Inside Beach to Outside Beach? It's a good place for
beachcombing and bird watching. Or try the foot trail around
Susan Lake. Just ask a local person, he or she will point you in
the right direction.

Seldovia is also justly famous for its profuse berries. Just head
off and go pick 'em!

The boat returns to Homer at 4:00 pm. Your evening is free.

As part of their passenger service, Rainbow Tours will arrange
an overnight stay at one of several bed and breakfasts or small
hotels in Seldovia. **Annie McKenzie's Boardwalk Hotel** (243
Main St., Seldovia AK 99663, 907-234-7816, deluxe price
range) and the **Seldovia Rowing Club** are especially picturesque. If you stay overnight, the *Sizzler* leaves for Homer at
7:00 am and again at 2:30 pm.

DAY 10
HOMER

Cross Kachemak Bay from Homer to China Poot Bay and spend
the day there. This trip, sponsored by the China Poot Bay Society, is a unique educational opportunity. Or saddle up for a day
trip up the beach to historic **Kilcher Homestead**. Your guide
and wrangler, Mariis (Mossy) Davidson, is a noted horsewoman
and breeder of Morgan horses.

Day 10 Suggested Schedule

8:30 am	Be at the office of Rainbow Tours on the Spit in the gray boardwalk, known as the Cannery. The tour leaves at 9:00 am.
12:00 noon	Picnic lunch in Peterson Bay or China Poot Bay.
6:00 pm	Time approximate. Return to Homer.
7:00 pm	Dinner.

Kachemak Bay Natural History Tour

Your captain aboard the *Sizzler* has developed a fine reputation for bird and wildlife spotting. On the way to Peterson and
China Poot Bays, the *Sizzler* stops by the bird sanctuary, Gull
Island. These rocky points sticking up out of the sea are home
to thousands of birds of several species, all living in harmony
and cacophony on this bird version of Mondo Condo. The boat
gets up close enough for some great shots of the birds and a
chance to view their lives and young. Fascinating.

Accompanying each China Poot Bay Society tour is a
volunteer naturalist who will show you the variety of life in this
area. The boat lands in China Poot Bay at the Society headquarters. Depending upon the tide, the tour goes from there to
three regions: (1) the tide pool at low tide (there is a 28-foot tide
in Kachemak Bay, one of the world's greatest); (2) the muskeg
swamp; and (3) the subarctic rainforest and hidden lakes. You
will also see an archeological site with the remains of a Denaina
Indian home.

Not only is this trip fun and very moderately priced, but part
of your fee goes to support the Center for Alaskan Coastal
Studies. There is a lot of walking on this trip, and the trail is
uncertain in places. Be sure to take rain gear, boots (there are a
few available at the Center), camera and film, and a substantial
lunch. Tea, coffee and cocoa are provided at the Center.

Day 10 Alternative
The day's trip begins at 9:00 am at Mossy's **Kachemak Seaside Farm** with a big Alaskan style breakfast. Then you saddle up the Morgan horses for a ride up the beach, stopping along the way to gather shells and driftwood, pick berries or photograph the fabulous scenery and maybe even a bald eagle's nest.

Stop in the afternoon at **Kilcher's Homestead**, a real, self-sufficient farm where Mossy was raised. The rolling hayfields, pastures and woodlands are ideal for hunting mushrooms, riding and berrying. Picnic lunch either along the way or at the homestead. Return by 5:00 or 6:00 pm.

The price of the trip includes, as a bonus, one night camping free at **Seaside Farm**, 5 miles out East Road from town. For more information, contact Mariis Davidson, Kachemak Seaside Farm, 58335 East Road, Homer, AK 99603, Tel. 907-235-7850.

If you love horses and the idea of exploring a piece of Alaska with a very knowledgeable Alaskan guide, this one-day trip can be expanded to 2 or 3 days. The itinerary will take you on past Kilcher's Homestead to Swift Creek near the head of the bay and to Mossy's charming Swift Creek cabin. This is an opportunity to relive the Alaska pioneer experience and also to get in lots of fishing, clamming and all-around Alaskan fun.

Day 10 Alternative	
9:00 am	Arrive at Seaside Farm for breakfast. Saddle up and depart.
5:00 pm	Return. This is a full day tour. The itinerary is somewhat variable depending upon the tide.

Wilderness Camping Option
If you crave a real backcountry wilderness experience, take the *Danny J.* ferry and, upon request, it will drop you at Glacier Spit, the gateway to 500,000-acre **Kachemak State Park** and adjoining parks. There are primitive camping sites with fire pits on the Spit. Stop by **Quiet Sport**, P.O. Box 874, Homer, AK 99603, Tel. 907-235-8620, and talk with proprietor, Dan Del Missier, who also has information on state and national parks, maps and supplies. The *Danny J.* will pick you up by prior arrangement on one of its regular runs.

This wilderness option could be all three days in Homer for those who want to hike and get into the back country. Cost of the trip to Halibut Cove is moderate.

Other Homer and Katmai Tour Options
Homer has so many things to do, you could spend the rest of

your vacation right here.

Kayaking is a popular sport in Kachemak Bay and Kachemak Bay State Park; however, due to rough and unpredictable seas and extreme tidal variation (as much as 28 feet), get some advice before you go do it. Dan Del Messier at **Quiet Sports** has lots of information, as well as kayak rentals. **Yaktreks** (contact through Dan) offers guided kayak trips.

With its miles of paved roads and incredible vistas, Homer is prime bicycling country. Bicycle rentals come and go in Homer. Check with Quiet Sports or the Log Cabin Visitors Center out on the Spit for bicycle availability.

An attractive alternative in Homer is a luxury getaway at Mike and Diane McBride's **Kachemak Bay Wilderness Lodge** in China Poot Bay. The prices are in the deluxe range, with full personal service and facilities. This lodge is consistently rated as one of the world's best wilderness lodges. Mike is a member of the prestigious Explorers Club and has more than 20 years' experience as a guide. The McBrides really know this area and its flora and fauna. Diane is an accomplished gourmet cook, and a sit-down meal in the main lodge room is a real treat. A five-day stay is recommended; however, to fit in with our itinerary, the McBride's will accommodate you for a 3-day stay if space is available.

Mike and Diane also operate **Chenik Wilderness Camp**, 100 miles southwest by air from Homer. The camp on Chenik Head faces Augustine Island volcano and is bordered by Katmai National Monument, the Valley of 10,000 Smokes. This awesome country has been vacant of human residents since prehistoric times. It is a place to photograph brown bear and much other wildlife. If you crave a true wilderness experience, this is it. Accommodations at Chenik Wilderness camp are available only as a 5-day package—arrival on Saturday and depart on Thursday.

Contact Mike and Diane McBride well in advance for reservations at either place: Kachemak Bay Wilderness Lodge, Box 956, Homer, AK 99603, Tel. 907-235-8910.
Today, leave Homer and retrace your steps to Anchorage with plenty of time along the way for stops.

If you've been dreaming about a raft trip in Alaska on a very fast paced but fairly smooth river, the Kenai could be it. Raft trips are available from several services along the river between Sterling and Cooper Landing. Inquire—the vendors change from season to season (see rafting information in the appendix). Expect that most trips will last at least several hours.

Get an extra early start out of Homer in the morning and catch up with the itinerary in Girdwood/Bird Creek tomorrow night.

DAY 11
BACK TO ANCHORAGE

Today, leave Homer and retrace our steps to Anchorage with
plenty of time along the way for stops.

Suggested Schedule	
8:00 am	Breakfast and good-bye to Homer.
9:00 am	Stop for some pictures at Stariski State Camp-ground, just north of Anchor Point.
12:00 noon	Picnic lunch.
3:00 pm	Stop at Portage Glacier Begich-Boggs Visitors Center for a one-hour
6:00 pm	Dinner in Girdwood/Aly. (You could leave Homer the previous evening and camp here. No fee. Water and restrooms.)

Trip Highlights
Head back up the Kenai Peninsula with stops along the way to
take in the sights, and maybe to do some clamming and fishing.
Twenty miles north of Homer and just past the town of Anchor
Point, pull off at Stariski State Campground. (You could leave
Homer the previous evening and camp here. No fee. Water and
restrooms.) This is one of the most beautiful campsites on the
Kenai. High up on the bluff, you look out directly on three
mountains in the Alaska Range: Augustine, an active volcano
which blew its top in March 1986 and is still smoking; next, Illiamna; and to your right, Redoubt. What a view! Photography is
mandatory.

   If you plan to fish, get an extra early start. The Ninilchik and
Anchor Point areas are home to king and silver salmon and
steelheads. Consult with one of the many fishing shops; the
waters here are closely regulated and off limits on some days.

   Clam Gulch has good clamming all the time. All you need to
try your hand at it are a shovel, a bucket, a low tide, and an
Alaskan fishing license. If you get some clams, cook them up on
the spot for lunch. At Soldotna, the route heads inland. The
Russian River is one of the most popular fishing grounds in
Alaska. The Kenai River is home to king and silver salmon.

   Turnagain Arm Inlet comes into sight once more. Make a right
turn at the sign for Portage, follow the road and keep looking to
your right. You will be rewarded by the sight of three glaciers,
flashing blue, descending from the mountains. The road ends
five miles later.

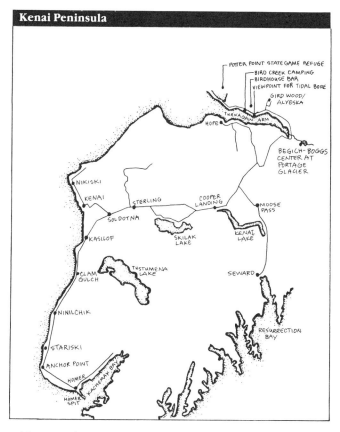

Kenai Peninsula

There are three Chugach National Forest campgrounds along this stretch of road. If you love the area, make one your home for tonight.

At Portage Glacier, tour the **Begich-Boggs Visitors Center**, which rests right on the edge of Portage Glacier Lake. There are hourly talks by forest personnel, and then a great movie on glaciers in the Center's stunning auditorium. Why can't all public works be designed as beautifully as this one? It looks out onto the lake, the glacier and icebergs carved off the face.

Retrace your steps to Highway 1, to Girdwood/Alyeska Resort and Ski Area. The community center, about 2 miles up the road at the turnoff to Girdwood, has picnic tables, pay phones, portable toilets and a playground. Make your dinner here, or eat out at what many feel is Alaska's best restaurant, the **Double Musky** in Girdwood, 907-783-2822. To reach the Double

Musky, make a left turn on Crow Creek Road. Double Musky is ¼ mile on your left. Owner-chef Bob Person uses Alaska seafood and Grade A beef to produce his prize winning Cajun/Alaskan cuisine, expensive but not outrageously priced. The combination of good service, excellent food and cozy ambience can't be beat. Try Blackened Redfish (done with salmon) or a big tender New York steak with bearnaise sauce. Don't miss the sinfully rich Double Musky fudge pecan pie.

An interesting phenomenon: when the tide returns twice daily into Turnagain Arm, it produces a "bore tide," that is, a great mass of water pushed through a narrow opening. The funnel of water can be as much as five feet high, although usually it is one or two feet. Time of the bore tide is posted at Portage Glacier Visitors Center. If the tide occurs while you are in the vicinity, the best vantage point is six miles from the Girdwood turn-off north on Highway 1.

On your left, a point of land extends into the water, and there is a pull-out. Park and take the trail, which is clearly visible, down to the water. Beware of going out on the rocks when the tide is coming in—you could get stranded. This tide moves fast.

Last stop on Highway 1 for the evening, 27 miles south of Anchorage, keep a sharp eye out to the right for a blue and yellow papier mache bird atop a small log cabin. The sign out front says "Liquor and Bar." The famous **Bird House Bar** is the most unique in Alaska, a tiny old log cabin, completely covered inside and out with business cards, pictures and memorabilia. One end of the cabin sank in the earthquake of 1964 and has never been raised. Seeing is believing!

Campers—turn in just up the road at Bird Creek State Campground, or in one of the many pull-outs just before the Bird House. If you need a room, head on into Anchorage or spend the night in the Girdwood area at the budget **Alyeska International Youth Hostel** on Alpina, Tel. 907-277-7388.

On your way into Anchorage, be sure to stop at Potter Point State Game Refuge, just before town. From the viewing platform, you can see up close an incredible assortment of 130-plus species of migratory birds. It is fantastic that this assortment of wildlife exists just a few miles from a major city.

DAY 12
ANCHORAGE

Take a day in Anchorage to resupply, go sightseeing, maybe catch a movie or some night life, before heading for the wide open spaces again. While in Anchorage, be sure to do any necessary maintenance work on the car—an oil change might be due after the long Alcan Highway drive—and stock up on groceries and personal items. Pick up a copy of the free Anchorage Visitors Guide, which can be found all over town, especially in hotels. It is loaded with information, maps, entertainment prospects and more. The Log Cabin Visitor Center, at the corner of Fourth and F Street, is loaded with information. There are pretty flowers and giant cabbages growing out in front.

People Mover Transit Center, on the southwest corner of 6th Avenue and G Street, offers cheap transport all over the Anchorage basin area, 7 days a week. Free downtown shuttle. Stop by for more information.

Suggested Schedule

8:00 am	Spend the morning taking care of any necessary chores and shopping.
12:00 noon	Lunch and your choice of the attractions listed below.
6:00 pm	Dinner. Evening free.

Sightseeing Highlights
▲▲▲**Anchorage Museum of History and Art**—121 West 7th Avenue at A Street, open 7 days, free admission, Tel. 907-264-4326, has a fine collection of contemporary art with a special focus on the American, and a large, permanent display on Alaska's unique cultural heritage.

▲**Fort Richardson Wildlife Center**—Located 9 miles north of Anchorage on Highway 1, near Fort Richardson, free admission. Lots of mounted animal trophies if you're interesting in that sort of thing.

▲▲▲**Earthquake Park**—At the west end of Northern Lights Boulevard, this spot was set aside to show the awesome effect on the land of the 1964 earthquake. It is not as dramatic as it used to be because trees and shrubs cover most of the upheaval. It's still a good place for a picnic, and on a clear day this is one of the best viewing spots (along with The Crows Nest at Captain Cook Hotel) from which to see Mt. McKinley and Mt.

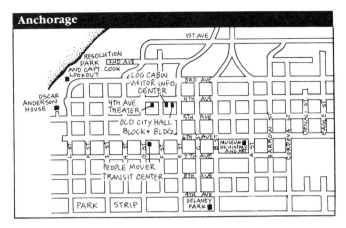

Foraker in the Alaska Range, which is to the north across
Knik Arm.

▲**Alaska Zoo**—Located south of town on Highway 1. Take
O'Malley Road east, two miles. Over 40 species of wildlife, including a musk ox, moose, reindeer and bears.

Kid Stuff: For children, Anchorage is a fun and exciting city.
There are parks all around the city streets and along the edges.
Some great things to see are the museum, the zoo, and Fort
Richardson—ask at the gate about having lunch in their
cafeteria, always interesting and inexpensive, when it is open to
the public. **Alaska Experience Theatre** will shake the kids
up. If there is time, visit the animal display on the ground floor
of the Alaska International Airport.

DAY 13

DENALI NATIONAL PARK

To travel from Anchorage 238 miles north to Denali National
Park, get an early start to allow for time in Talkeetna and a mid-
afternoon arrival at Denali which is crucial for securing camping reservations.

Suggested Schedule	
8:00 am	Breakfast.
8:30 am	Leave Anchorage.
10:30 am	Arrive in Talkeetna. Walk around town and have lunch.
12:30 pm	Back on the road.
3:30 pm	Arrive at Denali National Park.
3:30 pm	Orientation at Riley Creek Information Center. Get camping and hiking permits.
5:00 pm	Settle into your camper or room.

Travel Route: Anchorage to Denali National Park (238 miles)
Leaving Anchorage, follow Route 1 north 35 miles to the junction with Route 3, the George Parks Highway. Take the George
Parks Highway to Denali. Take the spur road to Talkeetna 14 ½
miles into town and then back up Route 3. Enter Denali National Park through the main gate for Riley Creek Information
Center.

Talkeetna is a cute little village of 600, located at the con-
fluence of the Talkeetna, Chulitna and Susitna Rivers. The name
Talkeetna means "river of plenty." As you enter town, you will
see a sign that says "Welcome to beautiful downtown Talkeetna." This is a small town with a sense of humor and it is full of
new wave, younger-generation Alaskan pioneers. Park when
you first get to town and then walk around. The whole village is
just a couple of blocks long and ends at Riverside Park.

Stop by the **Talkeetna Historical Society** museum on your
left, by the airstrip. The Society's annual fund raiser, the Moose
Dropping Festival, is held on the second Saturday in July.

Next stop is at the **Fairview Inn**, home base for many
assaults on Mt. McKinley. The bar is fun and funky.

Denali Dry Goods Store, housed in an old cabin, has an
interesting selection of camp craft, books and woolen sweaters.

It also offers a raft trip down the scenic Susitna River with Denali Rafts.

K2 Aviation, in a cabin just off the airstrip, has a one-hour McKinley sightseeing trip for a party of four for only $45 each. This is a good buy. If you don't have your own party of four, there may be others waiting to take the flight too who can join you to make a full party.

The **Talkeetna Roadhouse** is famous for its giant cinnamon rolls—one is a meal in itself. Across the street is a great Greek deli with souvlaki sandwiches, homemade baklava, and more.

You will probably depart Talkeetna with regret. It's a cute little place, whose unofficial motto is "The town where the women are good looking, the men are brave and the children are superior."

From Talkeetna to Denali the road is good and fast. Upon arrival at Denali National Park, head immediately for Riley Creek Information Center. This is important because by 4:00 pm during the peak season, from July 1 to mid-August, the park is often booked for the next day's registration for campsites.

Immediately pick up a copy of the *Denali Alpenglow* and get in line for a campsite. Be sure to read the next pages of this itinerary to understand which kind of campsite you should register for. Try to register the campsite for two nights.

To the right of the campsite reservation desk is the counter where you get your tokens for the shuttle bus; however, tokens are not available in advance; they are available only on the day you intend to use them, beginning at 5:45 am. There is also a desk for information on backcountry hiking and permits for backcountry camping. It is important to stop here if you intend to hike on your own. If you're extra lucky and manage to get a permit for tonight's camp, great. If not, you'll have to go to a public campground or a hotel. Settle in for the evening, read the *Alpenglow* and perhaps attend a lecture on the park—either at the campsite, where there are campfire lectures in the evening, or at the main hotel. Then, early to bed for an early start on tomorrow's incredible trip through Denali National Park.

No advance reservations are ever taken for a campsite at Denali National Park. You must appear in person and they are only good for that one night, or once those are sold out, for the next day ahead, unless you are planning more consecutive nights in the park. In that case, you can get permits for those nights when you make your initial registrations.

Denali National Park
The park has been set up to minimize visitors' impact on the fragile subarctic ecosystem. There are few trails outside the main entrance area, so hikers must disperse and thus lessen the

impact on the environment. Traffic is strictly controlled, with no access past mile 12 on the park road unless you have a camping permit for that night; even then, only one transit is allowed.

Most transportation is via park shuttle buses which ply the road, generally at half-hour intervals. To board at Riley, you need a token, free at the office. To board at other points, you don't need anything, just flag the bus down. However, to camp overnight within the park, you need a permit; for day hiking, you do not. This system makes it easy to get off when you want to explore on your own, on foot. Bear in mind that this is a real wilderness, and you are responsible for yourself! I suggest you read the free *Alpenglow* thoroughly and purchase at the Riley Creek Information Center a Denali National Park map for 25 cents and a copy of "How to Find Wildlife at Denali Along the Park Road", for $1.00. Consider buying *Denali National Park: An Island in Time*, by Rick McIntyre, an excellent, in-depth guide. When you get home, it makes a great souvenir or gift because of its glorious color pictures of the park and its inhabitants. Also, consider the *Denali Road Guide*, a mile-by-mile description of the road and its features. All the books, information maps, permits and reservations that you need are available at Riley Creek Information Center.

The park rangers are enthusiastic and very helpful. You should read the next section of this guide very carefully, and when you arrive at Riley Creek Information Center on the first day, make all reservations and obtain all permits you will need for your entire stay in the park, i.e., campsite reservations for one night, or all three nights, or as many nights as you will be spending in the park; the hiking permit (if needed) at the backcountry desk; and the overnight camping permit for nights 14 and 15 (13, too, if you're lucky).

Accommodations

Campgrounds: one night of free camping is allowed, for backpackers only, at **Morino Campground** by the train station, across from the Youth Hostel.

For those in camping vehicles, there are several pull-outs on the road just north of the park. Roadside camping within the park boundaries is strictly prohibited. The best commercial campground for easy access is **Lynx Creek**, located one mile north on the main highway from the entrance to the park. Generally, there is plenty of room. If this campground is filled, the **KOA Campground**, located farther north, always seems to have spaces.

For those who want a roof over their heads, the budget option is the **Youth Hostel**, located right by the train station. For an inexpensive room with shared bath, a tiny roomette in a converted railway car at **Denali National Park Hotel** is another low cost alternative. They also offer luxury accommodations. Another expensive but fun accommodation is **Denali Crow's Nest** (P.O. Box 700, McKinley Park, AK 99755, Tel. 907-683-2723), perched above the road just north of the main entrance. This convivial place has cute miniature cabins with room for 4 with two double beds. There are two large hot tubs.

Top of the line is **McKinley Chalet Resort**, a full-service resort with pool, sauna, recreation center which has nightly videos, a deli and an excellent and most scenic restaurant. Make reservations for either McKinley Chalet Resort or Denali Park Hotel c/o A.R.A. Outdoor Room, 825 West 8th Avenue, #240, Anchorage, AK 99501. Telephone numbers for reservations: in the park, 907-683-2215; in Anchorage, 907-276-7234.

Another alternative, available only on a four- or five-night stay, for those who have extra time, is **Camp Denali** (P.O. Box 67, Denali National Park, AK 99755, Tel. 907-683-2290), located at the very end of the National Park road in the geographical center of the park. This is a rustic, informal resort for those who seek the in-depth experience of a subarctic alpine wilderness. Accommodations are in individual guest cabins, located on a hillside with an expansive view of Mt. McKinley. Each is equipped with a wood stove for heat, pure spring water, propane lights, hot plate and a private "path." There are bathing facilities and a central shower, plus a hot tub. Delicious home-cooked meals are served family style in the central dining area. The comfortable living room has a large Alaskana library. The staff naturalist will help you maximize your experience at Camp Denali.

Food

If you're camping in Denali, you should have bought all your supplies in Anchorage. There are one tiny store and one gas station (expensive) near the information center. Be sure you have plenty of gas before driving in on the park road.

The snack shop at the **Denali Park Hotel** has inexpensive burgers and fries. Early breakfast, for 5:00 to 6:00 am departures, is available at Denali Park Hotel or **McKinley Chalet**. Prices are moderate; food service begins at 5:00 am. A giant breakfast buffet is available at **McKinley Denali Salmon Bake**; also, a bountiful lunch and an especially bountiful dinner. This is a good deal if you're hungry. McKinley-Denali Salmon Bake is located one mile north of the park entrance; Tel. 907-683-2733.

Lynx Creek Pizza at Lynx Creek Campground serves great pizzas at moderate prices.

Fine dining is available at **McKinley Chalet Resort**. Their jewelbox of a dining room overlooks the river, with a spectacular canyon view.

A good, quick meal, especially sandwiches, can be had at the **Denali Deli**, opposite the Chalet Resort, open 10:30 am to midnight—your best bet for a late night snack.

Healy Roadhouse, located 8 miles north of the park, is a traditional Alaskan stop for prime rib.

For those who plan to hike in the backcountry, be sure to read and observe the food handling rules published in *Alpenglow* to avoid a close encounter of the unpleasant kind with a local grizzly bear.

DAY 14

WONDER LAKE

A trip to Denali Park is the high point of any trip to Alaska. "Denali," an Athabascan word meaning "high one," was the Native American name for Mt. McKinley—at 20,320 feet, the highest mountain in North America, with the sharpest rise of any in the world. The park is the premier wildlife viewing preserve in North America. Thirty-seven kinds of mammals and 157 species of birds inhabit the park. With a little luck, you may see grizzly, moose, caribou, wolf and Dall sheep, among the larger mammals, all roaming free.

Suggested Schedule

4:30 am	Up and have breakfast. Pack a substantial lunch.
5:15 am	Be in line for a token which they start passing out at 5:45. The first shuttle bus leaves at 6. The earlier you leave, the better chance you will have of seeing wildlife and Mt. McKinley.
6:00 am	Shuttle bus to Wonder Lake. Lots of stops wherever you or your fellow travelers spot wildlife.
11:00 am	Arrive at Wonder Lake. Wow, what a view! Hike.
2:00 pm or later	Hop on the shuttle for the return trip. Again, lots of stops. Vehicles can only travel 35 mph maximum on the often one lane winding dirt road.
7:00 pm	Arrive back at Riley, or get off along the way for those who are backpacking and have a permit at a campsite tonight. For those who have a campsite and a vehicle, get your vehicle and head back to your campsite.
8:00 pm	Dinner and early to bed.

Denali Park Road to Wonder Lake
This is it—your chance to view this incredible wilderness preserve! Buses leave Riley Creek Information Center hourly, beginning at 6:00 am. The last departure that will leave time to return the same day is at 1:00 pm. The 85-mile trip to Wonder Lake takes 5 hours one-way. Stops along the way include Polychrome Pass, Toklat River and Eielson Visitor Center; the bus may also stop for wildlife viewing.

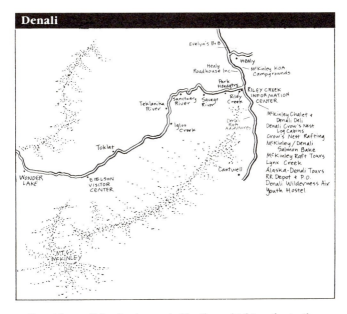

Consider walking back one-half mile and taking the trail marked "McKinley Bar Trail." Two miles each way, it is an excellent introduction to the beauty of hiking in the park. This trail forms the first leg of the Mt. Nearing route for climbing to the summit of Mt. McKinley. Have your picnic lunch.

The last return bus from Wonder Lake is around 6:00 pm, arriving back at Riley Creek at 11:15 pm.

DAY 15
HIKE DENALI

The Denali backcountry provides superb subarctic hiking. A full day of hiking can take you from tundra riverbanks, across meadows of alpine wildflowers, up into rugged glacial moraines—and back. There are virtually no trails in the backcountry. Most of the area is above timberline, and hikers usually follow rivers or ridgelines. A map is essential. Hiking permits are assigned on a zone system to prevent overcrowding of popular areas and to assure solitude for your wilderness experience.

Suggested Schedule

Spend the day hiking in Denali National Park.

Denali Backcountry
While riding the shuttle bus to Wonder Lake on the second day of your visit, watch for areas along the way that you'd like to explore further. The next morning, stop at Riley Creek Visitor Center, discuss your hiking plans with the ranger and get your permit. Then get on the bus and go do it!

If you don't want to brave it alone, discovery hikes depart daily. These are small group hikes, led by a park ranger/naturalist of four or five hours duration. The hikes are posted at Riley Creek. All you need to do is show up. They also post what you need, i.e., picnic lunch, extra shoes. Spend the rest of the day, before or after the hike, learning more about the park and seeing a sled dog demonstration at Park Headquarters. Demonstrations are held three times daily; times are posted at Riley Creek.

A raft trip is another possibility, as Denali is a favorite rafting area, with churning water (but not really all that rough) and great views. For complete information, contact **McKinley Raft Tours**, P.O. Box 138, Denali National Park, AK 99755, Tel. 907-683-2392. The tours are of various duration, several times a day. A family tour of 2 ½ hours, minimum age nine years, departs at 9:00 am and 2:30 pm. For the more adventurous, a tour which includes a fantastic stretch of white water, 22 miles total, departs at 9:00 am and 2:30 pm.

Flightseeing Mt. McKinley on a clear day is another great idea. Inquire at the train station, where there is a flightseeing company office.

DAY 16
DENALI TO FAIRBANKS

Fairbanks, known as "The Golden Heart of Alaska," is located on a flat alluvial plain near the geographical center of the state, about 100 miles south of the Arctic Circle. This is a friendly small city, worth several days' stay if you have extra time.

Suggested Schedule	
8:30 am	Leave Denali.
11:30 am	Arrive in Fairbanks. Take a walking tour.
12:30 pm	Go to the University of Alaska, Fairbanks, and visit the Geist Museum.
2:00 pm	Take a sternwheeler river excursion or spend more time sightseeing and shopping in town.
6:00 pm	Visit Alaskaland or Cripple Creek Resort for dinner and a show.
10:00 pm	The night life in Fairbanks is great. Go out and visit one of the clubs.

Travel Route: Denali to Fairbanks (120 miles)
Denali to Fairbanks is 120 miles north on Highway 3, a somewhat rough road. As you near Fairbanks, there are some glorious views of the Alaska Range to your right. Pull off for a picnic and enjoy the view.

Upon arrival in Fairbanks, stop at the Visitors Center at 550 First Street and take one of their hour long walking tours, or pick up a do-it-yourself walking tour brochure and walk around for an hour in the historic part of town.

Accommodations
Free camping is available at **Chena River State Recreation Site**, on University Avenue near the Chena River bridge or, for self-contained RVs, in **Alaskaland**. The **Tanana Valley Campground** (P.O. Box 188, Fairbanks, AK 99707, Tel. 907-452-3133), a fee campground, is centrally located on College Road.

For a roof over your head, the local B&B is **Fairbanks Bed and Breakfast**, P.O. Box 74573, Fairbanks, AK 99707, Tel. 907-452-4967, moderately priced. **Cripple Creek Resort**, just south of town, with shared baths, also has moderate rates.

Wedgewood Manor, 202 Wedgewood Drive, Fairbanks, AK 99701, Tel. 907-452-1442, is in a higher price range, kids free, continental breakfast included. This is a great place for families to clean up and let the kids swim. It has a pool, hot tub and

sauna, a big playground nearby, and a laundry. Accommodations are in one- and two-bedroom apartments, all with color
cable TV.

The Regency Fairbanks, 95 10th Avenue, Fairbanks, AK
99701, Tel. 907-452-3200, is an elegant small hotel in a convenient location. It's an expensive lodging choice. However, they
also serve excellent meals, including a high quality, all-you-can-
eat buffet breakfast and an all-you-can-eat soup and salad bar
lunch, both good bargains, especially if you take "all you can
eat" seriously.

Fairbanks Youth Hostel, P.O. Box 1738, Fairbanks, AK
99701, Tel. 907-479-4114, is located at Tanana Valley
Fairgrounds.

Food
Sunset Inn, 345 Old Richardson Highway, Tel. 907-452-4696,
is a local favorite, open for breakfast, lunch and dinner, with a
late night lounge.

A Moveable Feast, at Minne and Old Steese in Northgate
Square, Tel. 907-456-4701, serves croissants and good coffee, as
well as great sandwiches, soups, fresh pasta and desserts. It is
open for breakfast, lunch and dinner. Moderate.

The Pump House, Tel. 907-479-8452, offering fine quality
dinners in an historic setting on the Chena River, makes a great
spot to while away a summer evening, watching the boats go by.

But the best places for dinner during a short stay in Fairbanks
are **Alaskaland**, **Cripple Creek Resort** and **Gold Dredge
No. 8**. listed below as Sightseeing Highlights.

Sightseeing Highlights
▲▲▲**University of Alaska Museum**—On campus, open
daily, this small museum has excellent Alaska exhibits. Be sure
to see the movie of the Aurora Borealis, as well as the remains of
a 35,000-year-old-bison. There is a small entrance fee. Tel.
908-974-7505.

Across from the museum is a vantage point from which to
view the Alaska Range, with a map naming each of the peaks.
▲▲**Alaskaland**—Is Alaska's only pioneer theme park has no
rides, but lots of exhibits. In the evening there is an all-you-can-
eat salmon bake, followed by a comedy revue. Entrance to the
park is free; shows are inexpensive.
▲▲River Excursions—Alaskan sternwheelers leave daily at 2:00
pm for a 4-hour trip down the Tanana and Chena Rivers.
Departures are from Discovery Landing, near Fairbanks International Airport. For complete information, contact **Riverboat**

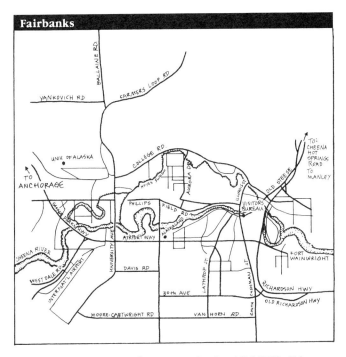

Discovery, P.O. Box 80610-TD, Fairbanks, AK 99708, Tel. 907-479-6673.

▲▲**Cripple Creek Resort**—A few miles south of town in Ester, P.O. Box 101, Ester, AK 99725, Tel. 907-479-2500. A theatre, a restaurant and a saloon are housed in old mining buildings. The resort features lots of atmosphere and a very good all-you-can-eat dinner, moderately priced. Nightly multimedia shows, with spectacular northern lights photography set to music, are staged by Photosymphony in the firehouse theatre. Later in the evening, there is a great comedy revue at the Malamute Saloon.

▲▲**Gold Dredge No. 8**—North of town in Fox, Alaska, this place offers a fascinating tour of an old gold dredge and a chance to pan for gold yourself. Excellent evening meals are served a la carte. The tour is inexpensive, meals moderate.

On your way out, notice the Alaska oil pipeline on your right . . .You can't miss it. Stop the car at the visitors parking area and read about the development of this incredible—and controversial—engineering achievement.

If you're a family vacationer, my kids inform me that **Alaska-**

land, **Cripple Creek Resort** and panning for gold at **Gold Dredge No. 8** are among their favorite places in Alaska.

Nightlife
A university town, Fairbanks has a lively nightclub scene. The **Pump House**, a local hot spot, features live entertainment, but no dancing. There are pool tables and a great view overlooking the river.

The Roof is a disco with a live band in the Entertainment Center on Airport Way at Marker, near **Alaskaland**. Also in the complex are bowling and skating. Nearby, a multi-screen theatre shows all the latest movies.

North Country Inn, a 15-minute drive north on the Steese Expressway in Fox, is where local people really let loose. There's dancing on the tables, and good food earlier in the evening.

Itinerary Option: Barrow
Here in Fairbanks, you're as far north as you can reach in Alaska by paved road, about 120 miles south of the Arctic Circle. A look at the map will show you that the route described in this book tours only the southeastern quarter of Alaska.

A second look will show why: there are virtually no other roads. It is impossible to reach the eastern part of the state by road, even in a 4-wheel-drive vehicle. The only road into the northern half of the state, the rugged unpaved James Dalton Highway, follows the Alaska Pipeline for 500 miles to Prudhoe Bay on the frozen northern coast; however, beyond the Brooks Range, the last half of the road is closed to the public. There are no towns or service stations along the Dalton Highway, and an expedition on this road as far as the Brooks Range would prove so demanding and time-consuming that your trip would soon cease to feel like a vacation.

If the inaccessibility of Alaska's far frontiers tantalizes you, there is one way to sample it within a reasonable vacation time frame. Fly. That's how residents of northern and eastern Alaska get around, and you can too. From Fairbanks, you can easily fly all the way to Barrow—the northernmost point in Alaska.

The "Top o' the World" is reason enough for many travelers to wish to go to Barrow, the world's largest Eskimo village, located 330 miles north of the Arctic Circle on the edge of the omnipresent arctic ice pack. The air is the purest in North America. The arctic winds blow away any pollution. For 82 days in the summer, May 11 to August 2, the sun never sets, and activity in town is continuous.

This is truly an exotic place, and not just because of its geography. The modern technological world and the ancient culture of the Eskimo collide here with strange effects. While modern society has made many inroads, the elders continue to pass along their traditional knowledge; and the durable, adaptable Eskimos seem to be progressing while maintaining their heritage.

As you stand on the windswept dark sand beach, you know that you are at the edge of the inhabited world—the top of the continent!

Suggested Schedule: Barrow Option

8:00 am	Have a big breakfast and plan to snack for lunch.
9:45 am	Check in at Fairbanks International Airport.
10:45 am	Depart. Snacks provided in flight.
12:00 noon	Arrive at Barrow. You will be met by your tour guide and bus.
2:00 pm	One hour free time to walk around town.
3:00 pm	Bus to Browerville for a stop at Mattie's Cafe.
3:30 pm	Bus to DEW Line (Distant Early Warning System), the northernmost tip of land.
4:00 pm	Town tour for a look at some of the strangest houses you ever saw.
5:20 pm	Return to airport. On the bus you will receive your Arctic Circle Certificate.
6:20 pm	Depart Barrow.
7:40 pm	Arrive in Fairbanks. What a day!

Barrow Tour

It makes sense to take a tour—individual round-trip air fare is more expensive. I recommend **Exploration Holidays Tour** from Fairbanks. Lee Hamme, a professional travel consultant in Fairbanks (530 7th Avenue, Fairbanks, AK 99701, Tel. 907-456-1906), who knows all the ins and outs, will make your reservation. Call ahead from Anchorage or Denali to assure yourself a space. Cost for a one day tour is $349.37, air fare and ground tour, buy your own lunch. An overnight tour is $423.37. Both prices include tax.

Dress warmly and casually when you leave Fairbanks. Wear several layers of clothing. Wear tennis shoes, and carry a spare pair, as the tundra is mucky. Bring a hat and scarf and maybe a candy bar or other high-energy snack.

Upon arrival at the airport in Barrow, your tour bus and guide will meet you. You'll bus into town to the Visitors Center, where you'll be provided with a parka to wear. (Yes, it's cold; about 35 degrees in the summer.) The bus will take you first to the bluff for an overlook of the area. Back at the Visitors Center, you'll see a dance performance, stories and folklore by a group of Eskimos, from the very young to the very old, a demonstration of crafts, an opportunity to buy them, and a traditional blanket toss. You hold the blanket.

The afternoon bus tour will take you to the DEW Line, the northernmost tip of Alaska, by way of Browerville, where you'll stop at Mattie's Cafe for the most unusual doughnut you ever ate, a look at the whalebone collection and a view of the communal village permafrost ice cellar.

I recommend the one-day tour but, for the avid photographer, an overnight tour, presenting a chance to photograph the full sequence of the sun which never sets, may be irresistible.

Barrow Restaurants
Pepe's at the Top o'the World Hotel in Barrow has some of the best Mexican food in Alaska. **Mattie Brower's Cafe** in Browerville, just across the little bridge, is your best bet for an Eskimo dinner, such as reindeer steak and stew.

DAY 17
FAIRBANKS TO KLUANE LAKE

Returning through Tok on your way to a late-night arrival at Kluane Lake, you will complete your Alaskan driving tour loop and find yourself southbound on the same road that brought you north 12 days ago. But this is not the last you'll see of Alaska. Instead, it is the first stage of a final long drive that will take you to Skagway for a leisurely three-day ferry cruise down Alaska's Inside Passage.

Suggested Schedule

8:00 am	Breakfast.
8:30 am	Drive Highway 2 to the Canadian border, 290 miles.
3:00 pm	Enter Canada.
10:00 pm	Arrive for the night at Burwash Landing, Kluane Lake.

Travel Route
From Fairbanks, follow Alaska Highway 2 the whole way. Just south of Fairbanks is the **North Pole**, a great stop for children. A giant Santa Claus marks the place on the highway. Kids: send postcards postmarked ''North Pole'' to your friends.

Road distances are 95 miles from Fairbanks to Delta Junction, 108 more miles to Tok Junction (where you turned off this highway on your way to Anchorage), and 50 more miles to the border. There, the highway designation becomes Canadian Highway 1. Continue to Burwash Landing on Kluane Lake. This means driving well into the evening; the farther you go tonight, the earlier you'll arrive tomorrow in the fascinating town of Skagway.

Accommodations
Burwash Landing Resort, Mile 1093, Alaska Highway, Yukon, Canada Y1A BV4, Tel. 841-4441, offers tent and van campsites, as well as moderate rooms. The restaurant features lake trout and, if you're lucky, sheefish. Say Hi to Ollie and Helen for me. In front of the resort is the **Kluane Historical Society Museum**, which you might visit before leaving in the morning.

If Burwash Landing Resort is full, 10 miles further south is the **Talbot Arms**, Tel. 841-4461, and 20 miles beyond that the **Bayshore Motel**, Tel. 841-4551. Both are in the moderate price range.

DAY 18
KLUANE TO SKAGWAY

The last driving segment of the tour covers 365 miles, climaxing with a spectacular trip down the Klondike Highway to Skagway, the port town of Alaska's gold rush days. The spirit lives on.

Suggested Schedule	
8:00 am	Breakfast.
8:30 am	On the road, driving along beautiful Kluane Lake.
1:00 pm	Arrive in Whitehorse.
2:00 pm	Begin a gorgeous drive on the Klondike Highway.
5:00 pm	Arrive in Skagway.

Travel Route
Haines Junction is a good place to gas up. **Mother's Cozy Corner Cafe** is a traditional stop for homemade pies. An hour after Haines Junction, look to your left in the tiny town of Champagne. There is an Indian cemetery with very well kept spirit houses. Please respect this sacred place and do not enter.

Stop in Whitehorse for shopping at the Yukon Native Products Store. Whitehorse is the place to buy picnic supplies for the ferry trip, if you haven't done so already.

Twelve kilometers (7 miles) past Whitehorse, you'll leave the Alcan Highway again, southbound on the Klondike Highway (Canadian Highway 2), which many people consider the most beautiful drive in the north country. You cross the border back into Alaska just before Skagway. Have your camera ready. You won't believe these vistas of giant waterfalls and shining emerald lakes. This is the place for a snowball fight, or a picture of you standing in the summer snow of Alaska. The town of Carcross is a well preserved town from the Klondike gold rush. Stop in town for a drink at the hotel. Fishing in Lake Bennett is fantastic for northern pike and arctic grayling.

Late in the day you'll arrive in Skagway. Go to the ferry office at the foot of Broadway and inquire if your ferry is on time; then, depending upon when your ferry leaves—tonight or tomorrow morning—check out historic Skagway. The town created by the gold rush to the Klondike in 1898 remains one of the best-preserved living tributes to that era. The town is small and good for walking.

Skagway Sightseeing Highlights
▲**Trail of '98 Museum**—Upstairs in City Hall, the museum displays fascinating gold rush memorabilia. Small entrance fee.
▲**Klondike Gold Rush National Historic Park**—The whole downtown Broadway stretch, seven blocks, is a national park. A free walking tour of the town is offered by the National Park Service Visitors Center, located in the old rail depot. Tours leave at 11:00 am and 3:00 pm. There are also free films and slide shows at the Center.
▲▲**Pullen Creek Park**—Out by the boat harbor, this is a nice spot for picnicking or fishing for pike and silver salmon.
▲**Molly Walsh Park**—On 7th Avenue, this small play park is great for kids.
▲▲**Skagway Overlook**—At Mile 1 on the narrow, winding Dyea Road, a turnoff with a wooden bench to sit on affords a wonderful view of Skagway below, on a clear day.
▲**Hiking Trails** abound near town. The trail to lower Dewey Lakes takes one hour round trip. The gold rush cemetery, 1 ½ miles from town, has fascinating old tombstones and makes a nice walk. Stop by the old train depot National Park Office for more suggestions on trails to hike.
▲▲▲**Skagway in the Days of '98**—The best of the gold rush shows, professionally done and great entertainment, plays nightly at 8:00 pm, as well as matinees, in the Eagle Dance Hall.

Accommodations
Golden North Hotel, Third and Broadway, P.O. Box 431, Skagway, AK 99840, Tel. 907-983-2294, the oldest hotel operating in Alaska, is furnished in original 1890s antiques. Relax in the restaurant and lounge. Expensive.

Skagway Inn in the historic district, P.O. Box 13, Skagway, AK 99840, Tel. 907-983-2289, has operated as an inn since the Twenties. All rooms are furnished in period style. Budget rates.

The **City Campground**, beside Pullen Creek, is convenient if you have a ferry to catch. Camping on the street in Skagway is forbidden. For a free campsite, drive out of town the way you came in. Just past the Dyea turnoff are pull-offs to the right by the river.

Food
Skagway has more than its fair share of excellent and entertaining restaurants. Starting from the top:

Irene's Inn, 6th and Broadway, is famous for its seafood and its captain's platter. Irene's also has an all-you-can-eat lunch and dinner buffet.

Prospector's Sourdough Restaurant on Broadway between 4th and 5th, Tel. 983-2865, is noted for its sourdough

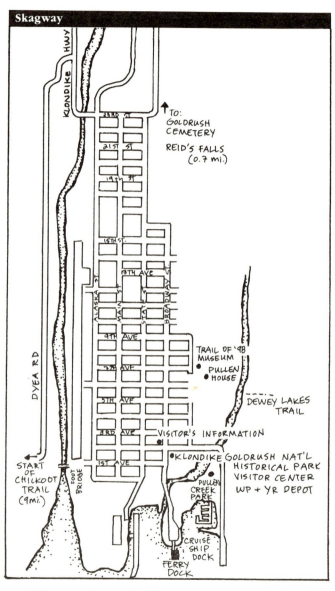

specialties, pancakes and waffles and its Italian meals in the
evening, especially the pastas, and good sandwiches
throughout the day. Prices are moderate.

The Sweet Tooth Saloon serves cafe fare in a turn-of-the-century soda shop environment. Excellent sandwiches.

Gold Miner's Pantry is a local bakery and hangout. They have fresh baked breads, pizza by the slice, chile and soup, and gigantic sandwiches. Budget prices.

The Cone Company, right on Broadway, serves ice cream by the cone. Many flavors.

The Red Onion Bar, on lower Broadway, near the docks, was a famous gold miner's saloon. It is still the most popular bar in town. There is often music—impromptu jam sessions as musicians come off the ship. A good stop for a sandwich and beer.

The lounge at the **Klondike Hotel** is a nice place to have a quiet drink. Floor shows in the Gold Rush style are featured on some weeknights. Another favorite local bar is **Moe's Frontier Bar**, a great spot for catching the feel of real Alaskan nightlife.

Itinerary Options
The Chilkoot Trail: If you can spend some extra time in the Skagway area, hike at least part of the Chilkoot Trail for a real taste of the gold rush! Through a 33-mile outdoor museum littered with relics of the past, the full trip is a 3-day hike.

The Chilkoot Trail is a historic backcountry trail, overseen by the National Park Service. There is a ranger station near the trailhead above Dyea, eight miles from Skagway.

You will need a good tent, able to withstand heavy winds, as well as hiking boots, rain gear, a backpack stove and warm clothes. Information and maps are available from the National Park Service at the old train depot in Skagway, or from the ranger station at the trailhead. Be sure to check in with the Park Service. For information and maps before you go, write to the Superintendent, Klondike Gold Rush National Historic Park, P.O. Box 517, Skagway, AK 99840.

This is a fabulous, though arduous, hike. Due to often severe and unpredictable weather conditions, it is not one to be undertaken lightly. On a 3-day hike, the first night's stop should be at Sheep Camp, just before the steep grade, so that you can start fresh in the morning. On the second night, camp either at Deep Lake or Lindeman City. (In the spring of '98, it was a tent town with 10,000 inhabitants!)

You must pre-clear Canadian customs by calling 403-821-4111. Contact *Gray Line* in Skagway for their schedule so that you can get a ride back to Skagway at the end of the trail at Log Cabin. *Atlas Bus Service* at 983-2402, and *Yukon and White Pass Bus Service* at 983-2241 in Skagway have service from Log Cabin back to Skagway. Call them in Skagway before you leave, and remember that Log Cabin in the Yukon is one hour behind Alaska time.

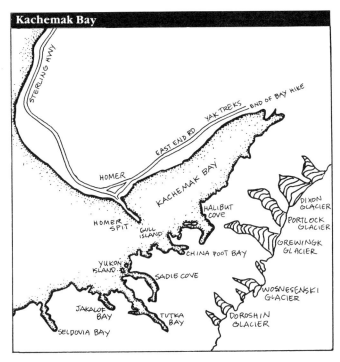

Kachemak Bay

STERLING HWY

EAST END RD.   YAK TREKS   END OF BAY HIKE

HOMER

KACHEMAK BAY

HOMER SPIT

GULL ISLAND

HALIBUT COVE

DIXON GLACIER

PORTLOCK GLACIER

GREWINGK GLACIER

CHINA POOT BAY

YUKON ISLAND

SADIE COVE

WOSNESENSKI GLACIER

JAKALOF BAY

TUTKA BAY

DOROSHIN GLACIER

SELDOVIA BAY

Haines Eagle-watching: The Chilkat River Bald Eagle Sanctuary, near Haines, has a fall and winter gathering of 3,500
eagles, the largest congregation known, drawn by annual chum
and coho salmon run.

There are more bald eagles, national symbol of the U.S., in
Alaska than in all the other states combined. The bald eagle
population in Alaska is estimated at 40,000. It is easy to see why
these magnificent birds, with their wing span of six to eight feet
and distinctive white heads and tails, were chosen as the symbol of the USA. Soaring overhead, the eagle is grace in motion.
Eagles mate for life and build huge nests, up to eight feet wide
and seven feet deep, which are elaborated upon each year.
Eagles have an unusually long lifespan, at least 50 years. The
exact time is not known. They are birds of prey and scavengers
who eat mostly fish and small rodents.

In Haines, the spacious and moderately priced **Ft. Seward
Bed and Breakfast**, House No. 1, P.O. Box 5, Haines, AK
99827, Tel. 907-766-2856, overlooks the parade ground and
beautiful canal; snow-capped peaks tower in the rear. A large,
comfortable inn with original woodwork, veranda and tile

fireplaces, it was once the former Chief Surgeon's quarters.

Except during the eagle gathering, I do not recommend joining or disembarking from the ferry at Haines. The town has little to recommend it and the road from Haines Junction to Haines (Canadian Highway 3/Alaska Highway 7) is one of the worst in the highway system. Instead, get on the ferry in Skagway.

Other prime eagle-watching spots on this itinerary include the shores of Kachemak Bay near Homer and the southeastern region around Ketchikan's misty fjords.

POST-TOUR OPTION
GLACIER BAY

If you have extra time, the best way to improve upon this 22-day itinerary is to explore more of gorgeous southeast Alaska. If I had an additional week, I would opt to spend most of it in the environs of Glacier Bay. Although this is not an inexpensive trip, it's well worth the price and is one you will never forget.

Glacier Bay, a short flight from Juneau, is one of Alaska's most important and interesting destinations. Here, sixteen massive glaciers converge on a narrow waterway: a thundering spectacle, the likes of which you won't find elsewhere.

The itinerary I suggest is:
- Disembark from the Ferry at Juneau.
- Spend two days in Juneau exploring this lovely town with its magnificent setting and Mendenhall Glacier.
- Depart on the evening of the second day, at 4:30 pm, for Gustavus.
- Spend Days 3, 4 and 5 exploring Glacier Bay, by kayak or by day trip from Gustavus.
- Return to Gustavus on the evening of Day 6 to catch the flight back to Juneau.
- Day 7, rejoin ship.

You could approach this trip in several ways: as a do-it-yourself camping and kayaking trip, with the assistance of *Glacier Bay Sea Kayak*, P.O. Box 26, Gustavus, AK 99826, Tel. 907-697-2257; or as an all-inclusive guided and outfitted kayaking and camping trip from *Alaska Discovery*, 418 South Franklin Street, Juneau, AK 99801, Tel. 907-586-1911; or as one or more day-trips while making your headquarters at the **Gustavus Inn** or **Glacier Bay Country Inn**. Or you could fit one of Ronn Storro Patterson's biological journeys into your trip plan.

NOTE: To make this trip, you need to coordinate your ferry departure times carefully. To visit Glacier Bay, you will need to make arrangements to get off the ferry in Juneau and board again, a week later, for the trip south.

Kayaking to Glacier Bay
Here is a sample itinerary for a 5-day do-it-yourself kayak trip in Glacier Bay. The guided kayak tours follow a similar route.

Day 1: Spend the morning and afternoon exploring the many sights of Juneau. Board the afternoon flight at 4:30 pm (arrive at the airport by 3:30) on Alaska Air Lines to Gustavus. The plane arrives in Gustavus at 5:00 pm. 6:30 to 7:30 pm: orientation to the area and the equipment. 7:30 pm: load your kayak on the *Thunder Bay*. Spend the evening at the campground or at **Glacier Bay Lodge**.

Day 2: Depart from Bartlett Cove on the *Thunder Bay* at 8:00 am. A half-day cruise on the park tour boat will take you to a remote area in the Muir Arm of Glacier Bay. Campers and kayakers are dropped off there at midday. Pack up the kayak and explore the long, sandy beaches. After a picnic lunch around 1:00 pm, kayak to the face of McBride Glacier. Make an evening camp on McBride Glacier, South.

Day 3: After breakfast, paddle north toward Riggs Glacier. After lunch, depart from the Riggs area and head up toward Muir Glacier, the most remote glacier in the Muir Arm. There will be good opportunities to observe seals on icebergs. Kayak southward along the opposite shore for your evening campsite.

Day 4: A leisurely morning paddle brings you to Wolf Point, a good place for a hike along dividing ridges or dividing beaches. You will have opportunities to observe marine mammals and bird life, or a possible cliff-side eagle's nest.

Day 5: After breakfast, make a final exploration by kayak or on foot. Late in the morning, the tour boat will pick you up at Wolf Point for a cruise that provides a dramatic overview of the whole Muir Inlet.

Return to Bartlett Cove in time to catch the bus to the airport, then the Alaska Air Lines jet to Juneau.

Gustavus and Glacier Bay the Easy Way

For those who don't fancy spending a few days camping and kayaking, I would heartily recommend spending a few days at Gustavus Inn or Glacier Bay Country Inn. Both offer two- or three-night packages that include an all-day boat tour aboard the *Thunder Bay*, the same boat that takes campers and kayakers in and out.

Other things to do in and around Gustavus include riding bicycles (provided by the inn), beach hiking, taking a guided nature walk in Bartlett Cove; and taking a day kayak trip in Bartlett Cove. World-class fishing is found in Glacier Bay's icy straits.

Gustavus Inn, Box 31, Gustavus, AK 99826, Tel. 907-697-2254, started in 1928 as a homestead for a large family of settlers. Today, the inn offers attractive and comfortable rooms as well as delicious meals of local seafood and produce. Bicycles and fishing equipment are available. All meals are included. Rates are moderate.

Glacier Bay Country Inn, Box 5, Gustavus, AK 99826, Tel. 907-697-2288 is an idyllic homestead that blends old-fashioned country comfort with the wilderness of Alaska—a fisherman's dream, traveler's paradise and professional's retreat. Guests enjoy cozy rooms, fresh local seafood and freshly-baked bread. Moderate rates.

Natural History Expedition

Glacier Bay, or any of several other remote destinations in Alaska, can also be visited on a one-week biological journey, which can be slotted handily into your itinerary by disembarking from the ferry in Juneau, Petersburg, Sitka or Ketchikan, depending upon the trip you wish to take. Biological journeys are full-scale whale watching and natural history expeditions aboard the *Delphinus*, a fully-equipped, warm and cozy 50-foot ocean-going motor vessel.

Ronn Storro Patterson, a naturalist and marine biologist, is one of the founders of the Whale Center. Ronn and his wife, Judy, conduct one-week trips through southeastern Alaska to such destinations as Misty Fjord National Monument, Glacier Bay and Icy Strait, as well as Frederick Sound, prime humpbacked whale territory.

Ronn is a walking encyclopedia. He and Judy do everything to make your trip a learning experience you will never forget. Contact **Biological Journiers, Inc.**, 1876 Ocean Drive, McKinleyville, CA 95521, Tel. 707-839-0178.

Humpback Whales of Southeast Alaska

Humpback whales are perhaps best known for their songs. Herman Melville said of them, "He is the most gamesome and light hearted of all the whales, making more gay foam and white water generally than any other kind of them." Melville was right. Perhaps less well known is how few of these whales there are. In the north Pacific there are perhaps as few as twelve hundred left—strictly a remnant of the original population that was literally decimated by recent industrial whaling.

The most acrobatic time for humpbacks is the summer, when they are busy feeding. It is then that southeast Alaska becomes so important for them. In just one small portion called Frederick Sound, as many as three hundred humpbacks have been individually identified. Another population center is Icy Straits. Still others inhabit specific passages, straits and canals. All together, there might be as many as 500 humpbacks using southeast Alaska as their principal feeding area—or nearly one half of the entire remaining north Pacific population.

—Ronn Storro-Patterson

DAY 19
THE INSIDE PASSAGE

Spend the final days of your Alaska trip cruising the Inside Passage. The Marine Highway System is a unique and wonderful way to experience some of America's most striking scenery. The exact itinerary for these days depends on which ferry you're taking and its route on that run.

The Alaska Marine Highway System

The "Blue Canoes"—ships of the Alaska Marine Highway fleets—are a familiar sight in southeast and south central Alaska. Each of the nine ships is modern, well equipped and very efficiently run.

Our trip aboard the Marine Highway System begins at Skagway. I highly recommend boarding in Skagway, rather than Haines. Historic Skagway is a lot more fun, and the trip from Whitehorse to Skagway is one of the most sensational in the north. Haines, on the other hand, has little to recommend it— aside from the nation's largest congregation of bald eagles in late summer and fall—and the road between Haines and Haines Junction is one of the worst in the highway system.

At present, there are two northbound sailings per week from Seattle to Skagway, and two southbound sailings per week from Skagway to Seattle. If you wish to book a stateroom, it is imperative that you do so as early as possible. Reservations for the forthcoming season open on the first work day in January. However, should you find that the staterooms are all booked, you can request to be placed on the standby list. You have a good chance of getting a stateroom. They are very reasonably priced.

There are three classes of staterooms: family rooms, rooms suitable for just a couple, and men's and women's dormitory accommodations. Budget travelers frequently take deck space, a viable alternative as the upstairs solarium is mostly enclosed and fitted out with chaise longues that lower to full reclining position, astroturf and heat lamps. The strategy, for those taking deck passage, is to be ready to board the ship as early as possible, make a dash for the solarium and stake out your chaise longue. If you are not lucky enough to get a chaise lounge, be sure to have a mat to put down on the astroturf-covered deck. There is usually no problem in obtaining a deck passage ticket without a reservation; however, reservations are a good idea.

Meals in the restaurant, served cafeteria style, are generally very good. Fresh Alaskan seafood is featured. If you are on a budget, take a substantial picnic basket aboard and rely on the cafeteria for hot drinks and an occasional splurge.

You are allowed to take aboard as much as you can carry—
officially, three pieces of luggage. You are also allowed to bring
aboard, free of charge, a bicycle or a kayak, which you must
carry on.

One big plus in traveling the Marine Highway System is the
convivial atmosphere aboard. There are lots of impromptu card
games, guitar playing and sing-alongs in the solarium, and a
generally nice feeling. Each ship carries about 600 people.

Fares: Deck passage southbound, Skagway to Seattle, is
around $200 one way.

Children's fares are: ages 5 and under, free; 6 to 11, one-half
fare; 12 and over, adult fare.

A cabin that will accommodate 2 persons is $191 with win-
dow, $168 without.

Unfortunately, the price to transport your motor vehicle is
high. Vans of 15-19 feet cost $575, in addition to passenger fare.

Cruise Ship Alternative

Although many cruise lines ply the waters of the Inside Passage,
only one fits in with this itinerary: the Admiral cruise ship, *Stardancer*. The *Stardancer* is unique in that it is a quite luxurious
full-service cruise ship with two car decks so that you can drive
your car, van, or RV right on board. Accommodations are in
staterooms.

It is possible to take *Stardancer* from Vancouver to Skagway,
or from Skagway south to Vancouver. The northbound trip
takes three days and runs from $615 to $1100 per person, plus a
port tax of $25. The southbound trip takes four days and runs
from $815 to $1465 per person, plus $30 tax. Although the
cruise is not cheap, it definitely falls into the "affordable luxury" class. For a family with children and a vehicle, *Stardancer*
can work out to be not much more expensive than a ferry, and
it is a wonderful way to end your trip.

For reservations, write to **Admiral Cruises**, P.O. Box 010882,
1220 Biscayne Boulevard, Miami, Florida 33101, or call
800-327-0271.

Cruising the Inside Passage

Ferries leave at different times depending upon stops and tides,
so I can't suggest an exact schedule.

Stopovers are all too brief, most averaging 1-1/2 hours. The
length of the stop will be announced as you enter port.
Generally, buses or taxis meet each incoming ferry in Juneau,
Ketchikan and Sitka to take passengers into town and bring
them back. However, going into town is really only possible if
the stop is for 1-1/2 hours or more. You may disembark from
the ship completely and re-embark another day. You will be

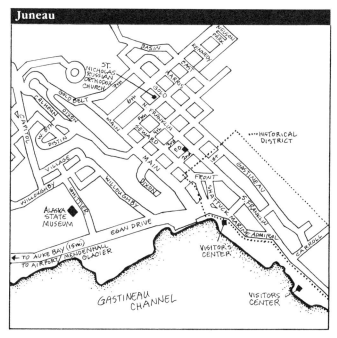

charged a point-to-point fee, which is only slightly higher than the through fare. I have included brief lodging, restaurant and sightseeing recommendations for those who wish to take advantage of one or more stopovers along the way.

Based upon a morning departure from Skagway, the ferries stop at Haines about 1-1/2 hours later.

Upon departing Skagway, you cruise **Lynn Canal**, a very steep-sided fjord which terminates in Chilkoot Pass. The area flattens out as you approach **Haines** and the Chilkat River Valley. The area is noted for timber, fine fishing and, in the late summer and fall, many bald eagles.

The ferry stops in the afternoon of Day 19 in **Auke Bay, Juneau**, a densely forested area backed by 5000-foot peaks of the Boundary Range. Mendenhall Glacier licks out from the vast Juneau ice field.

Juneau

Juneau is Alaska's capital and its third largest city. Its dramatic setting on Gastineau Channel, at the base of Mt. Roberts, and its proximity to Mendenhall Glacier, make Juneau a favorite stop.

Transportation
Juneau has two ferry terminals. The city terminal is right in
town. Auke Bay Terminal is 15 miles northwest. A mini-bus
meets the ferry at Auke Bay and provides inexpensive transport
into town.

Accommodations
Juneau Hostel, 614 Harris Street, Juneau, AK 99801, Tel.
907-586-9559, is a new facility ideal for the budget-minded
traveler. The hostel features small dormitory-style rooms for
men, women and families. There is a common area with
fireplace, as well as laundry and cooking facilities.
    Mullins House, 526 Seward Street, Juneau, AK 99801, Tel.
907-586-2959, is a Bed and Breakfast in downtown Juneau,
reasonably priced. The Victorian ambience will charm you, and
the special breakfasts will tempt you. It's a good base from
which to visit galleries, restaurants and the theater.
    Louie's Place, P.O. Box 704, Elfin Cove, Juneau, AK 99802,
Tel. 907-586-2032, is in the moderate price range. Discover the
spirit of Alaska in the picturesque village of Elfin Cove. Relax on
the porch swing; pick blueberries in the front yard, and treat
yourself to some of the best fishing in Alaska.
    Tenakee Inn, 167 S. Franklin, Juneau, AK 99801, Tel.
907-586-1000, is a beach-front Victorian near a natural hot
spring. The inlet offers views of whales and seals, as well as
good fishing. Hiking, hunting, kayaking and cycling are all
available nearby. Moderately priced.
    The **Juneau Bed and Breakfast Association**, Tel. 907-
586-2959, offers comfortable accommodations in various local
houses at moderate prices.

Juneau Sightseeing Highlights
▲▲**Alaska State Museum**—The museum has a large collection of Alaskan native artifacts. The upstairs exhibits are from
the Russian period. Free.
▲▲**St. Nicholas Russian Orthodox Church**—The stained
glass and the icons evoke Russian times here. Admission $1.
▲▲▲**Mendenhall Glacier Visitors Center**—What a
sight! The Visitors Center has films, slides, and a relief map of
the area.

Restaurants
Breakfast and lunch at the **Fiddlehead Restaurant and
Bakery** feature vegetarian food in a warm and delightful
atmosphere.
    Armadillo Headquarters, a local hangout on South
Franklin Street, downtown, has excellent Mexican food. Mex-

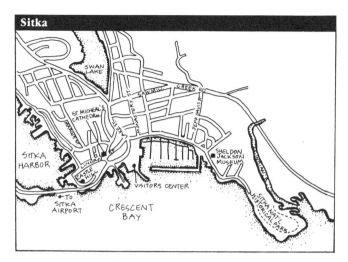

ican restaurants and fast food places are your best bet for an inexpensive meal in Juneau.

The Salmon Bake at Gold Creek, and **Thane Ore House**,
both a short distance from town, offer free bus service from
Marine Park in their marked vans. Mid-range prices for all you
can eat.

Ferries which leave Skagway in the evening stop at Haines later
the same evening. They arrive and depart from Juneau during
the first night. During the transit from Juneau to Sitka around
Admiralty Island, keep a lookout for Point Retreat lighthouse.
As you cross Peril Strait, a very narrow channel where the
shoreline is close, keep a lookout for deer and bear on shore as
well as whale and porpoise in the water. This is another prime
wildlife viewing transit.

Sitka

Sitka enjoys a stunning setting by the Sitka Sound, and faces Mt.
Edgecumbe, a classic, cone-shaped volcano. Onion-domed St.
Michael's Cathedral dominates the city's skyline, a reminder of
Sitka's Russian past.

Transportation

The ferry docks 6-1/2 miles from town. There is a shuttle bus to
town. A tour bus meets the ferry and takes you to most of the attractions. Both buses are budget-priced.

Sitka Sightseeing Highlights
Sitka National Historic Park—Walking around this unique
100-acre park, complete with a 2-mile walking trail lined with
many totem poles, is an excellent way to spend your time in
Sitka. The park is a 10-minute walk from downtown. If you do
opt to visit Sitka National Historic Park and walk the trail, that's
probably all you will have time for during the short ferry stop
in Sitka.

▲**Castle Hill**—On this National Historic Site (formerly the site
of four Russian castles, all destroyed), Old Glory was first raised
over Alaska in 1867.

▲▲**St. Michael's Cathedral**—Contains a priceless collection
of Russian ecclesiastical treasures. $1.00 donation.

▲▲**Sheldon Jackson Museum**—On the campus of Sheldon
Jackson College, the museum contains an extraordinary collection of Indian and Eskimo art.

DAY 20
THE INSIDE PASSAGE

On the second day aboard, the ferry makes a short stop at Petersburg. You cross the Kaku Inlet, which is a major salmon spawning river. The area is heavily forested with Sitka spruce, hemlock, and, along the shoreline, alder.

Between Petersburg and Wrangell are the Wrangell Narrows. In traversing these very narrow channels, the ship comes as close as 100 yards to shore. This is one of the best areas on the entire trip to spot deer and bear on shore as well as whale and porpoise in the channel. The ship stops briefly at Wrangell and then makes a longer stop in the afternoon at Ketchikan.

Keep a sharp eye out, as you near Ketchikan, for the totem poles on Totem Bight, north of town.

Ketchikan
Ketchikan means "thundering wings of an eagle stream," an apt name for a town built around fabulous salmon-spawning streams. Ketchikan boasts several things. It is Alaska's first (southernmost) city. Known for its rainfall, which averages 150 inches annually, and its king salmon run, said to be the largest

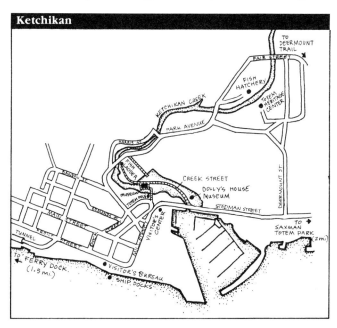

Ketchikan

in the world, the city is surrounded by Tongass National Forest, the largest in the U.S. These superlatives aside, Ketchikan is a fascinating town with much Tlingit and Haida Indian culture in evidence, most notably, the totem poles.

Most ferries stop in Ketchikan for only two hours. Cruise ships often stop for four hours.

There are two areas worthy of exploration. Either one can be explored in two hours. The ferry docks north of the older part of town are where most of the interesting sights are, convenient for a walking tour; or take a taxi to the **Tongass Historical Museum**, which houses a collection of native art and culture. The front is a good one for photos.

Ketchikan Walking Tour

Begin the walking trip by taking the bridge near the museum over Fish Creek stream and onto the boardwalk, which is Creek Street.

Follow along with a possible stop at **Morning Raven Gallery**, a shop with work by local artists, including some T-shirts with fanciful fish motifs.

Next stop, at No. 24, is **Dolly's House**, a step back in time to the 1920s, when Dolly entertained fishermen. There is a small entrance fee.

Fish Creek deadends in Dock Street. Go left to Deermount Street, left on Deermount, up the steep hill to the entrance to **Totem Heritage Center**, $1.00 admission. This collection of 33 original totem poles is unsurpassed. The brief talk given by the guide is fascinating. The building is in the style of a Tlingit long house. The unique traditional designs on the T-shirts sold in the museum shop can be found nowhere else. Behind the Center is the **Deer Mountain Fish Hatchery**, which also makes an interesting stop. You can usually join a tour in progress.

Depending upon your time of departure, either retrace your steps and catch a taxi back to the ferry on Dock Street or, if you have a bit more time, take the trail on the creek at the fish hatchery to Park Avenue. Go left on Park. The walk goes by the river through an old part of town. On your left will be a fish ladder, an amazing sight when the fish are running (July through October). Park runs into Bawden Street. Go left to Dock Street and catch a taxi.

For those with extra time in Ketchikan, The 3.1 mile trail up the mountain, which begins near the city landfill and a mile from downtown, offers a panoramic view of Ketchikan and surrounding islands from the 3000-foot peak.

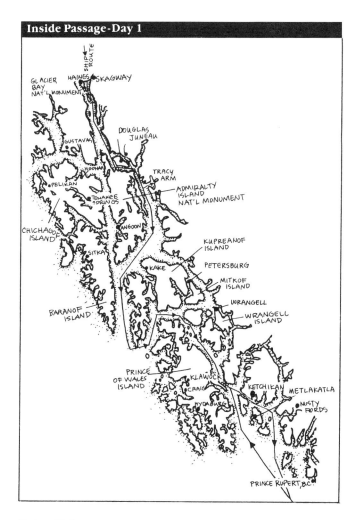

Inside Passage-Day 1

Totem Poles

Another interesting possibility for Ketchikan sightseeing is to take a taxi to **Saxman Totem Park**, six miles south of town. The Saxman poles have been assembled from all over Southeast Alaska, and some have been made by artisans working at the site.

Totem poles, carved from long-lasting red cedar, are up to 60 ft. in height. The totem is the figure at the top. The signs and symbols on the pole pertain to the tribes and their history. The poles have profound social and religious significance, however they are not worshipped. Different artists within a tribe portray the traditional animals and symbols differently. There are some clues to identification. Certain forms were used by almost all of the artists. A bird will have claws, a beak, or wings. A raven's beak will be straight, long and narrow. Sea mammals or fish will have a fluted tail or fin. The beaver, with large incisor teeth, is usually seen holding a stick in its front paws. Bear or wolf will have a pointed nose, large teeth or claws. Frog and halibut are easily recognized. Although some designs are hard to identify, their resemblance to symbols carved on rock in Northern Peru is very noticeable. Poles were erected to celebrate births, tribal events and potlatches. Others were memorials to dead chiefs, erected by their successors, and some memorial totem poles contain the cremated remains of the person they memorialize. These would be held in a small box in a niche in the pole.

The poles were not meant to last forever. An average life-span would be 70 years. Poles commemorating potlatches bear a ring for each potlatch the chief has given. However, rings were never added to the poles; instead, a new pole with the additional ring would be erected. Color was used on the poles only to pick out the details. A copper-bearing clay made the highly prized blueish-green color. From ochre came browns, yellows and reds. White was made from clam shells and black from graphite or manganese.

A bonus highlight of a trip to Saxman is the opportunity to see the Cape Fox dancers perform. This internationally-renowed troup of 60 dancers puts on an extraordinary perform-ance, highly evocative of Tlingit culture. Close your eyes and you can almost smell the wood smoke in the long house and imagine the potlatch in progress. Find out before you go if the Cape Fox dancers will be performing by calling 225-9038, or the sales desk at the Ingersoll Hotel, 225-2124. If the dancers are not going to perform, then I suggest taking the walking tour instead. If you have more time, Ketchikan would be a good place to get off the ferry for a day or two.

Accommodations
The newly renovated **Gilmore Hotel**, 326 Front Street, Tel. 225-9423, is a charming and elegant (and expensive) place to stay, evocative of Ketchikan's picturesque past.

Five local houses that offer reasonably priced B&B accom-modations can be booked through **Ketchikan Bed and Breakfast**, P.O. Box 7735, Ketchikan, AK 99901, Tel. 225-3860.

The **Rainforest Inn**, 2311 Hemlock St., Tel. 225-9500, offers hostel-style accommodations—both a large dormitory and private rooms that accommodate two to four people, 3/4 mile from the ferry terminal. It's a friendly place. Hostelers of all ages can also contact **Ketchikan Youth Hostel**, Box 8515-7D, Ketchikan, AK 99901, Tel. 907-225-3319.

Food
Harbor Light Pizza, 2531 Tongass Avenue, serves great pizza. **New Peking**, 4 Creek Street, offers Chinese food in a wonderful setting overlooking Creek Street. Prices are moderate at both places.

   June's Cafe, Stedman and Creek Street, makes chili that will warm you through and through. **Gilmore Garden**, 216 Front street, presents seafood and other good meals in an elegant setting.

   McDonald's, serving well, you know is near the ferry in Plaza Port West Mall. **First City Cookies**, Nirvana for the chocolate chip crowd, is at 217 Main St.

Nightlife
If you're in town on Friday night, be sure to catch the performance of the **Fish Pirate's Daughter Melodrama**, one of the best shows around and an all-Alaska performance.

   Frontier Saloon features straight-on rock 'n roll; **Pioneer Bar** and the **Rainbird Bar**, country music; **Thunderbird**, music and dancing. **Gilmore Gardens** is the place for a late night espresso and pastry.

DAY 21
THE INSIDE PASSAGE

On the third day aboard, there are no stops as you cruise the lower portion of the Inside Passage. The scenery on all sides is stunning. The water may get a little choppy later in the day, as the ship traverses a section of open ocean between Queen Charlotte and Vancouver Island. Port Hardy, on the northern tip of Vancouver Island, is one of the world's largest lumbering sites.

On the morning of the fourth day, you'll arrive in Seattle.

Inside Passage-Day 2

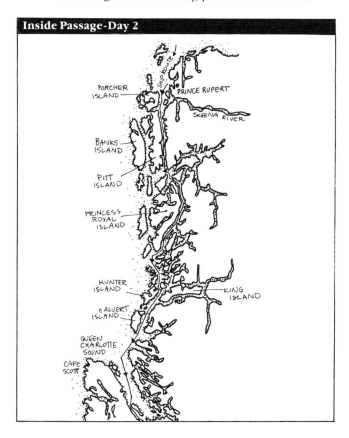

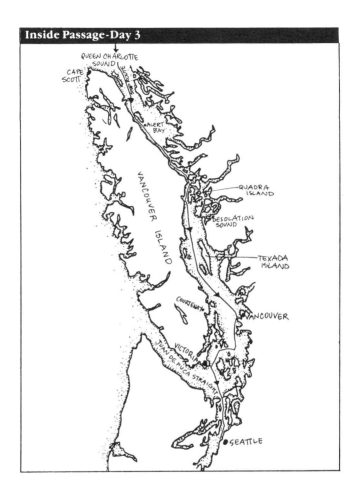

Inside Passage-Day 3

QUEEN CHARLOTTE SOUND

CAPE SCOTT

ALERT BAY

VANCOUVER ISLAND

QUADRA ISLAND

DESOLATION SOUND

TEXADA ISLAND

COURTENAY

VANCOUVER

VICTORIA

JUAN DE FUCA STRAIGHT

SEATTLE

DAY 22
SEATTLE

The ferry docks right in the heart of the Seattle waterfront at Pier 48. A comprehensive guide to Seattle sightseeing is beyond the scope of this book. Upon arrival in Seattle, you'll probably want to take a rest day on terra firma before starting the journey homeward. Here are a few suggestions for spending a day in the waterfront area.

Suggested Schedule

Breakfast 7:00 or	Aboard ship.
8:00 am	Ship docks. Disembark.
9:00 am	Park your vehicle and walk to Pioneer Square.
10:00 am	Take the 90-minute Underground Tour.
12:00 noon	Take a bus or walk to Pike Place for lunch.
2:00 pm	Seattle Aquarium.
4:00 pm	Go along the piers and pick up your vehicle.

Transportation
For those disembarking the ferry with a vehicle, there is all-day parking one block from the pier at the Old Seattle Garage on Jackson Street.

For those traveling deck passage, you can stow your things in lockers at the pier while you explore Seattle.

Getting around Seattle is easy. Everything on our itinerary can be reached by walking. (After being aboard ship for a few days, it feels good to walk around.) City buses are free in the central downtown area; just hop on. The antique trolley car that runs up and down Alaskan Way paralleling the waterfront costs 25 cents.

Sightseeing Highlights
▲**Underground Tour of Pioneer Square Area**—A fun, off-beat 90-minute walking tour of Seattle underground. The city's streets were raised one story above ground level to get them out of the mud of the original "Skid Road." The subterranean tour of old downtown Seattle is unique and quite entertaining. Tours run all day, from 10:00 am. They leave from Doc Maynard's Public House, 610 First Avenue. The cost is $3.50. Reservations are recommended; call 206-682-4646. Just across the street from Doc's, you can pick up the bus for Pike Place Market.
▲▲**Pike Place Market**—This historic waterfront market

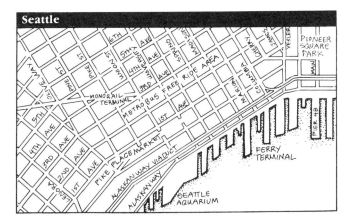

pulses with life all day. Stop by for lunch and last minute shopping. Fresh seafood, packed to travel, is a good Seattle purchase.

▲▲**Seattle Aquarium**—Fascinating displays of underwater life make this a ▲▲▲ stop if your children are with you. One of the highlights is the 180-degree view in the underwater dome. It's located on Pier 59, open 10:00 am to 7:00 pm daily. The **Museum of Sea and Ships** is also located at Pier 59. Moderate admission is charged at each.

Food
Try **Pure Food Fish Market**, 1511 Pike Place, Tel. 206-622-5765. They have smoked fish too. Enter Pike Place at Pike, First Street entrance. There are a number of food stalls and small stores within the market where you can get lunch.

The Old Spaghetti Factory, at the corner of Elliott and Broad, Tel. 206-441-7724, serves giant plates of pasta—bring an appetite.

McCormick & Schmicks, 1103 First Avenue, Tel. 206-623-6500, has fabulous seafood!

Nightlife
Seattle nightclubs abound. Take a tip from Pamela: **The Comedy Underground**, 222 South Main Street at Swannies, Tel. 206-628-0303.

Accommodations
Hotel Alexis, 1007 First Avenue, Tel. 206-624-4844, just a few blocks from the pier, is elegant and expensive. There is a lovely restaurant, as well.

Emerald City Inn, 1521 Belleview, Tel. 206-587-6565, is a charming guest house, a short ride from the pier. Rates are moderate.

Budget lodging can be found at the **Y.M.C.A.** (Co-ed), 909 Fourth Avenue, Tel. 206-382-5000.

Airport Transport
Driving, take James Street, which connects to I-5, southbound for the Seattle airport. If you need transportation, pick up *Gray Line Airport Express*, which runs every 20 minutes from the Four Seasons Olympic Hotel at 411 University, a few blocks from Pier 48. The trip takes 40 minutes. Tel. 206-624-5813. Or, you can take the city bus #174, or #194, the Express. It runs along Second Avenue and Stewart Avenue, and will take you aboard with any luggage you can carry. Depending upon the time of day, the trip takes 30 minutes to one hour. Metro Bus information: 206-447-4800.

FISHING, RAFTING & SHOPPING

Alaska offers leisure activities for every taste. Here are a few of my favorites:

Fishing

It's true! The fishing in Alaska is better than almost anywhere else on earth. Fish abound in inland streams, lakes and coastal waters. Only glacial streams, heavy with rock flour, offer poor fishing. Let this whet your appetite: 300-pound halibut caught frequently in Kachemak Bay. Or, how about a 90-pound, hard-fighting king salmon? Or, maybe a 45-pound lake trout? Fish for salmon, grayling, turbot, pike, arctic char, Dolly Varden, rainbow and lake trout, sheefish, bass, whitefish, snapper and halibut.

Salmon have been the staff of life of the coastal north country since prehistoric times. Their dependable, annual run from the sea to spawn in clear water streams provided early people with a reliable food source, readily obtained in the summer and preserved for the winter. Thus they had the leisure time to develop a complex culture.

There are five species of salmon in Alaska: King Salmon, which grow from 15 to 50 pounds and run from June to mid-August, have dark brown, red brown, or black bodies. They can produce more than 7,000 eggs and they spawn mostly in the large rivers. Pink salmon, also known as humpback, or humpies, are three to five pounds. They run in July and August. Their coloration is dark brown on the back with a white underbelly. They swim close together in dense schools and spawn in tidal waters. Coho salmon grow from eight to 10 pounds and have a dark red-brown body. Red salmon, also known as the sockeye are a spectacular bright red with a green head. And finally, chum salmon, the favorite of Alaska's ursine population. Salmon are anadromous. They spawn in clear fresh water, the eggs hatch after four to six months and the young, called smolts, migrate to the ocean to mature. When full grown, in two to four years, salmon return to the stream of their birth, sometimes a journey of more than 1,000 miles. Swimming against rapids up the stream, they spawn and die. So the cycle continues with marvelous dependability, as it has for at least two million years.

The salmon population has declined, due to over-fishing in the Twenties and Thirties and perhaps due also to logging and mining pollution. Hatcheries all over coastal Alaska now rear millions of baby fish, known as "fry," with the aim of increasing the salmon population. Studies show that it is working.

Go clamming for butter clams, abalone, razor clams,

geoduck, and mussels so big and succulent you won't believe it.
Note: Clams and mussels can be dangerous if eaten during a red
tide. Check with a local source to make sure they are safe to eat.

Octopi are found under rocks at low tide. And what about
giant geoduck, 15-pound mollusks dug from tidal flats? The accepted method of digging them is to spot a hole at extremely
low tide, especially in the Kachemak Bay area where the tidal
variation is 28 feet. Anyway, find a hole made by the leg of a
geoduck. Quick, plunge your hand into the mud, grab the
geoduck by its foot; have your accomplice dig like crazy. About
three feet down you'll find your prize. Fun, but dirty.

If you're over 16, you'll need a fishing license in Alaska.
These are available in sporting goods stores and roadside lodg-
ings in fishing areas. These people offer good advice, too, on
local hot spots and know the many local fishing regulations. A
14-day license for Alaska is $20. A 5-day Canadian license runs
$10.

The Alaska Department of Fish and Game has two useful
booklets and a map, available free: "Alaska Sport Fishing Regulations and Summary" and "Sport Fishing Predictions." Send for
them to: Alaska Department of Fish and Game, Box 3-2000,
Juneau, Alaska 99802.

Throughout this itinerary, I've mentioned the excellent
fishing opportunities along the way. However, for the avid
fisherman looking for the ultimate experience, rumor has it that
fishing in the Kuskokwim area in the central part of the state
just can't be beat. Write: George and Kathy Morton, Morton's
Fish Guiding, Red Devil, Alaska 99656 for details on their all-
inclusive rustic fishing trips. Good fishing!

Rafting
Rafting opportunities in Alaska are unsurpassed. A wide variety
is available, from gentle, scenic trips to whitewater runs.

In the itinerary, I've made note of rafting possibilities in Lyt-
ton, B.C., on the Kenai Peninsula, in Talkeetna and the
Denali/McKinley area. If you're keen on rafting, be sure to get
the book *Floating Alaskan Rivers* by M. Carter, $6.95, pub-
lished by **Nova Riverunners of Alaska**, P.O. Box 444-WG,
Eagle River, AK 99577. Nova Riverunners also sponsor many
rafting trips.

Shopping
Shopping in Alaska runs the gamut from throw-away tourist
junk to contemporary art treasures. Even if you just want to take
home a few souvenirs and gifts and perhaps buy something
special for yourself, you are sure to find things you'll love. What
follows are my recommendations:

Some of the best shopping in Alaska, isn't; it's in the Yukon. The **Yukon Native Products** store in Whitehorse, 4230 Fourth Avenue, Whitehorse, Yukon, Y1A 1K1, Tel. 403-668-5955, features distinctive native products made the traditional way with pride in workmanship. There are excellent buys on beaded moosehide moccasins, lined or unlined, many home-tanned by age-old methods and redolent of wood smoke. (I saw identical moccasins in Alaska for more than twice the price!) Men's, women's and childrens' sizes are available. There also is a wide assortment of water-repellent Cowichan sweaters, caps and gloves, hand-spun and knitted by the Cowichan people. These quality woolens are among the best Canada has to offer.

Another specialty is paper birchbark baskets at great prices. The **Kluane Museum Shop** has a selection of beaded moosehide moccasins and beaded jewelry.

The best selection of gold nugget and jade jewelry is in Anchorage. My favorite shop is **Wiona's**, right down the street from the Visitors Log Cabin. They have some fabulous antique pieces, at fabulous prices, and the best of the new work. Gold nugget jewelry is available all over Alaska and it's best to buy this expensive item from an established jewelry and gift shop. In Fairbanks, out at the **Gold Dredge No. 8**, there is a tiny gift shop with a resident goldsmith producing lovely new takes on turn-of-the-century designs in gold and silver.

While in Anchorage, be sure to stop by Ooming Mak, **Musk Ox Pioneers Adventure**, 604 N Street, the only place to buy genuine musk ox Qiviut knit goods. This exquisite wool knits up into a scarf fine enough to pass through a wedding ring. A true luxury item.

Homer has some excellent shopping. **Alaska Wildberry Products** has wildberry jams, jellies, butters and fruit drinks from the local pick. Take your selection with you, or they will mail the berry goodies for you. They also have a very wide selection of T-shirts, sweat shirts and inexpensive jewelry.

Toby Tyler sells boxed note cards of Alaska wildflower paintings and fine prints, all at good prices.

Ptarmigan Arts has some very high quality and unusual art and crafts by local artists: beautiful handwoven jackets, pottery with Alaskan motifs, sculpture, painting, and more. Much of it is more au courant in design than other Alaska fare.

Velma Katch Canning out on the Spit, will send the folks back home a case of Alaskan-smoked seafood—your own catch if you're lucky—always a winning gift.

Talkeetna has extra fine handcrafts by modern-day pioneer/ artisans—wonderful things like leather clothing in current styles, moccasins with quality soles, knives and hand knits.

Denali/Mt. McKinley is home to one of my favorite shops in

the **McKinley Chalet Resort**. The best of everything, from all over the state. McKinley T-shirts and sweat shirts are knockout gifts.

Skagway has some of the best shopping in the whole state and is the best place for your last minute purchases before the trip back.

Some inexpensive gift ideas: gorgeous Alaskan calendars; boxes of notecards, depicting Alaskan people, animals and wildflowers; Moose dropping geegaws—corny but fun; black plastic jewelry with tiny gold flecks embedded in it—striking; T-shirts; and jars of Alaskan berry jam and jelly. Little genuine jade and ivory jewelry pieces can be had for under ten dollars. Most Alaskan establishments give away matchbooks. Pick them up as a gift for your friends who collect!

PUBLIC TRANSPORT TO ALASKA

It is possible to follow this itinerary traveling to Alaska without a vehicle. Our trip is put together of modular pieces, which can be rearranged to fit your means of transport. The cost of transportation on the 22-Day itinerary is about $700 per person.

By Bus: Greyhound from Seattle to Vancouver is $19.95 one way. There are several departures daily from Eighth Avenue and Stewart Street for the 4-hour trip. Phone: 206-624-3456.

Greyhound, Vancouver will take you to Whitehorse for $129 Canadian, one way. Service most days, leaving at 8 am, and arriving 2 days later at 5:45 am Sleep aboard. Stops at roadside diners for meals. Phone: 604-662-3222.

White Pass-Yukon coaches have service from Whitehorse to Anchorage, 800-544-2206 and 907-277-5581, or in Whitehorse, 403-668-6665 ($135 US). The bus departs at 12 noon, arriving at 7:30 pm the next night. Stay overnight in Beaver Creek on the Canadian side. There is a KOA campground, as well as Ida's Motel. Service from Whitehorse or Skagway is twice weekly. Anchorage to Whitehorse or Skagway is twice weekly. The same bus, which is a flag-stop service, (you can flag down the bus on the road) coordinates schedules with the Alaska ferry system for a morning departure from Skagway, arriving around noon in Whitehorse. The fare from Skagway to Anchorage is $178 US. For advance schedule, write Gray Line of Alaska, 300 Elliott Avenue West, Seattle, Washington 98119. You may fly from Anchorage to Homer for about $69 on ERA Airline, 907-243-6633, Anchorage, or 800-426-0333.

Alaska-Denali Transit also has bus service to Homer. Phone: 907-276-6443 in Anchorage.

From Anchorage to Denali and Fairbanks, there is bus service aboard Alaska-Denali Transit; daily departures arriving in Denali in the early afternoon, then on to Fairbanks. The trip from Anchorage to Denali is $35; from Anchorage to Fairbanks, $55. Alaska-Denali Transit has a very special trip about twice a month in the season, to the Arctic Ocean. Call them for information. Alaska-Denali Transit also has passenger van service from Anchorage to Haines, and Haines to Anchorage to meet the ferry. Cost is $100 per person. You will be accommodated in one of several reasonable hotels.

By Train: There is Anchorage-Denali-Fairbanks service on the Alaska Railroad. Reservations: 800-544-0552. One-way to Fairbanks, $90. Departures daily from 411 West First Street, Anchorage. The train leaves about 8 am for the 6½ hour trip to Denali, then goes on to Fairbanks where it arrives in the early evening. The train ride is a gorgeous trip, and a beautiful way to get there. The food aboard the train is excellent.

By Ferry: Both north and southbound. Taking deck passage on the Alaska Marine Highway System is a fine way to make your way north and south. The ferry leaves Seattle twice a week. If you are unable to obtain deck passage (unlikely), or a cabin (likely) on the Alaska Marine Highway System from Seattle, your chances are much better from Prince Rupert. Call ahead. There are four weekly sailings from Prince Rupert.

But first, you must get there. Bus from Vancouver via Greyhound, $106.15 Canadian, one way. Phone: 604-662-3222. It makes the 25-hour trip daily.

Another advantage of the ferry is that you can get off and on the ferry at points of interest in Southeast Alaska to spend a day, or a few days, and get back on the ferry. You will be charged point-to-point fare, which is slightly higher than a straight through fare. See our heading under Alaska Marine Highway System for more information.

By Airplane: United has a low-price, advance-purchase fare for $397 round-trip, Seattle-Anchorage. Phone: 800-241-6522.

Delta Airlines, 800-THE-WEST, has some advance-purchase tickets, Seattle-Fairbanks, which allow for stops in Juneau and Anchorage. This fare is sometimes called the Midnight Sun Express, and is currently about $686 round trip.

Alaska Airlines, 800-426-0333, has service to most Alaskan cities.

14-DAY HIGHLIGHT TRIP TO ALASKA BY PUBLIC TRANSPORTATION

DAY 1 Fly to Anchorage. Take a morning flight, as early as possible to maximize your time. Rent a car immediately upon your arrival, having reserved it by phone beforehand. There are car rental agencies at the airport. Spend the afternoon and evening exploring Anchorage.

DAY 2 Drive to Homer. Today you'll cover 225 miles at a leisurely pace southwest to Homer. Our route, along Turnagain Arm and down the Kenai peninsula, offers fabulous scenery at every turn. Arrive in Homer at 3:00 pm, and make reservations and preparations for the next two days activities in the area. Evening free.

DAYS 3 & 4 Please see all choices in our main itinerary Days 8, 9 and 10, and in Alternative Days 8, 9 and 10 for myriad ideas for things to do in Homer. This is the best place in our itinerary to get out and experience Alaska.

DAY 5 Today you leave Homer and slowly retrace your steps to Anchorage with stops along the way at Stariski to view the incomparable Alaska Range at Portage Glacier Begich-Boggs Visitors Center, and to enjoy an early dinner at the lovely Girdwood Alyeska area. Camp for the night at Bird Creek just outside of Anchorage or return to town to a Bed and Breakfast or hotel.

DAYS 6 & 7 Rise and shine early for your train to Denali. Train departs early in the morning and arrives early in the afternoon. See suggestions in 22-Day itinerary Day 13, 14 and 15, for ideas of things of do on Day 7 in Denali, but I would recommend taking the bus trip to Wonder Lake and back. While you're out there, why not take the hike along McKinley Bar Trail.

DAY 8 Morning in Denali. Take the afternoon train back to Anchorage, arriving around dinner time.

DAY 9 Board the bus for the trip to Skagway. Travel through a beautiful part of Alaska and spend the night in a hotel at the border, or camp.

DAY 10 Rise and shine for your trip through the Yukon, finishing up at Skagway.

DAY 11 Board ship for the return south through the Inside Passage.

DAYS 12, 13 & 14 Cruise through the Inside Passage, per the main 22-Day itinerary Days 19 through 22.

DAY 14 Arrive in Seattle.

You can shave a day off this itinerary and spend it somewhere else—perhaps one more day in Denali or in Homer—by flying from Anchorage to Skagway to meet the ferry, instead of spending two days driving through Alaska and the Yukon; however, the trip through Alaska and the Yukon is truly incomparable— very beautiful, very wild, and highly recommended.

It is important, when planning this 14-Day trip, to work around the departure date of the ferry from Skagway south, and make your reservations accordingly. *All* your reservations should be made from the lower 48. If I were taking this trip, before leaving home I would:
■ reserve a car to be picked up at the Anchorage airport;
■ reserve a Bed & Breakfast for the first night in Anchorage;
■ make my train reservations to and from Denali;
■ make my bus reservation to Skagway and, of course,
■ make my ferry reservation.

HOSTELS

Founded in 1934, American Youth Hostels (AYH) provide simple, safe overnight accommodations for traveling members, regardless of age. Memberships are available from American Youth Hostels membership services, 1332 "I" Street NW, Suite 800, Washington DC 20005, or from the hostel itself. The initial membership fee is about $20. Hostel accommodations are available to non-members on a members first availability basis. Currently, the maximum hostel charge is $9, and many hostels charge much less. Certain customs pertain to hostels in general.

Check-in time is 5:00 to 8:00 pm. Curfew ranges from 10:30 pm to 12:00 midnight and is posted in the hostel. Most hostels are closed from 10:00 am to 5:00 pm. A small housekeeping chore is a daily duty. Smoking is not allowed within the hostel. Alcohol and drugs are prohibited. Accommodations are in separate male and female dorms. A few hostels have family sleeping rooms available.

Home hostels require the utmost courtesy as you are in someone's private home. Hostelers must bring their own sheet sack or sleeping bag. There is a 3-night maximum stay.

Hostels provide the lowest cost accommodations for travelers who don't camp.

For more information on Alaska Youth Hostels, contact The Alaska Council, P.O. Box 91461, Anchorage, Alaska 99509, Tel. 907-264-2120.

Hostels in Alaska include: **Fairbanks Youth Hostel**, P.O. Box 1738, Fairbanks, AK 99701, Tel. 907-479-4114. Location: Tanana Valley fairgrounds. Open June 1 to September 1.

Delta Youth Hostel, P.O. Box 334, Delta Junction, AK 99737, Tel. 907-895-4627. Location: 3 miles from Milepost 272, Richardson Highway. Open June 1 to September 1.

Tok International Youth Hostel, P.O. Box 532, Tok, AK 99780. Location: 1 mile south of Mile 1322.5, Alcan Highway. Open June 1 to September 1.

Susitna Ranch Youth Hostel, Box SRA 650, Willow, AK 99688, Tel. 907-733-2775. Location: Mile 101.8 Parks Highway. Open summers only.

Anchorage Youth Hostel, P.O. Box 49226, Anchorage, AK 99509, Tel. 907-276-3635/276-9522. Location: Minnesota Drive & 32nd Ave. Open all year.

Alyeska International Youth Hostel, P.O. Box 10-4099, Anchorage, AK 99510, Tel. 907-277-7388. Location: near Alyeska Ski Resort on Alpina, in Girdwood. Open all year.

Soldotna International Youth Hostel, P.O. Box 327,

Soldotna, AK 99669, Tel. 907-262-4369. Location: 444 River-
view Drive. Open all year.
   Snow River International Hostel, P.O. Box 8, Moose Pass,
AK 99631, no telephone. Location: Mile 16, Seward Highway.
Open all year, starting July 1, 1986.
   Sheep Mountain Lodge, SRC Box 8490, Palmer, AK 99645,
Tel. 907-745-5121. Location: Mile 113.5 Glenn Highway. Open
May 1 to October 31.
   Bear Creek Camp & Hostel, Box 334, Haines, AK 99827,
Tel. 907-766-2259. Location: Small Tract Road, 2 miles from
town. Open all year.
   Juneau Internation Hostel, 614 Harris St., Juneau, AK
99801, Tel. 907-586-9559. Location: 4 blocks NE of the Capitol.
Open all year.
   Sitka Youth Hostel, Box 2645, Sitka, AK 99835, Tel.
907-747-8356/747-6332. Location: Methodist Church,
Edgecumbe & Kimsham Sts. Open June 1 to September 1.
   Ketchikan Youth Hostel, P.O. Box 8515, Ketchikan, AK
99901, Tel. 907-225-3319. Location: United Methodist Church,
Grant & Main St. Open June 1 to September 1.

BED AND BREAKFAST

B&Bs along the itinerary route are listed in the respective Days. If you get off the beaten path, you may wish to visit one of these B&Bs:

Favorite Bay Inn, Box 101, Angoon, AK 99820, Tel. 907-788-3123, moderate. A rambling, comfortable inn overlooks the boat harbor at the entrance to Favorite Bay on Admiralty Island, an area rich in wildlife. Guests receive family-style Alaskan hospitality in a beautiful setting.

Reluctant Fisherman, Box 150, Cordova, AK 99574, Tel. 907-424-3272, moderate. Great fishing, hiking and sightseeing are easily accessible from your harbor-front inn at Cordova, a community on Prince William Sound in the Gulf of Alaska. "Flightseeing," hunting and fishing charters are available.

B&B Valdez, 3346 Eagle, Box 442, Valdez, AK 99686, Tel. 907-835-4211, moderate. You'll feel right at home in this friendly, relaxed and comfortable setting. Enjoy the antique furnishings and the complete dedication to your comfort and enjoyment.

Totem Inn, P.O. Box 648BB, Valdez, AK 99686, Tel. 907-835-4443, luxury. A family-owned inn with a true Alaskan atmosphere. Enjoy modern rooms with cable TV and telephones, full breakfast and an Alaskan wildlife display.

Heger Haus, 1216 Nordic Drive, Petersburg, AK 99833, Tel. 907-772-4877, luxury. Heger Haus, a converted boat building warehouse, has been transformed into a country-style inn overlooking Alaska's famed Inside Passage. Full country gourmet breakfast for the hungry traveler.

Scandia Haus, P.O. Box 689, Petersburg, AK 99833, Tel. 907-772-4281, moderate. Scandia Haus, a venerable 80 year old establishment, is the original and only hotel in Petersburg. Clean, comfortable rooms feature satellite TV and telephones.

Afognak Wilderness Lodge, Seal Bay, AK 99697, Tel. 907-486-6442, luxury. Enjoy the rustic elegance of a remote forest and fjord paradise. The adventure starts when you are dropped off via float plane, and it continues with delicious meals featuring fresh local seafood and wild game.

ALASKA FAIRS AND CELEBRATIONS

Alaska is a land with special celebrations the year round. Following is a comprehensive list of fairs and celebrations during the months in which we recommend traveling.

MAY
Chamber Honors the Arts—Anchorage, date varies.
Viennese Waltz Night—Anchorage, early part of the month.
Gulkana Air Show—Gulkana, third weekend.
Nenana River Daze—Fairbanks, end of month.
Spring Art Festival—Homer, date varies.
Snowbirds Air Show—Juneau, mid-month.
Salmon Day—Ketchikan, third Saturday.
Salmon Derby—Ketchikan, fourth Saturday and Sunday.
Ocean Race—Ketchikan, May 2.
Little Norway Festival—Petersburg, mid-month.
Salmon Derby—Sitka, fourth Saturday and Sunday.
Victoria Day Weekend—Skagway, mid-month.
Miner's Day—Talkeetna, third weekend.
King Salmon Derby—Wrangell, most of the month.

JUNE
Alaska Women's Run—Anchorage, date varies.
Basically Bach Music Festival—Anchorage, mid June.
Mayor's Midnight Sun Marathon—Anchorage, summer solstice.
Midnight Sun Hot Air Balloon Classic—Anchorage, summer solstice.
Renaissance Faire—Anchorage, second weekend.
Kite Day—Anchorage, June 1.
Campbell Creek Classic—Anchorage, date varies.
Nalakatak Whaling Festival—Barrow, date varies.
Tanana Raft Classic—Fairbanks, first weekend.
Flying Lions Airshow—Fairbanks, first Saturday.
Midnight Sun Baseball Game—Fairbanks, summer solstice, June 21.
Summer Solstice Festival—Fairbanks, third weekend.
Yukon 800 Classic—Fairbanks, third weekend.
Riverboat Race—Fairbanks, third weekend.
Bike Race—Fairbanks, date varies.
King Salmon Derby—Haines, first weekend.
Homer Halibut Derby—Homer, date varies.
Juneau Public Market—Juneau, end of month.
Salmon Derby—Ketchikan, first, second and third weekends.
Nenana River Daze—Nenana, first weekend.
Salcha Country Fair—North Pole, date varies.

All Alaska Logging Championships—Sitka, end of June or early July.
Sitka Summer Music Festival—Sitka, Tuesday and Friday all month.
Salmon Derby—Sitka, first weekend.
Writers Symposium—Sitka, mid month.
Summer Solstice Party—Skagway, June 21.
Nuchalawoya Festival—Tanana, date varies.
All Alaska Pioneer Stampede—Wasilla, date varies.

JULY
Fourth of July—Alaskans tend to be super patriotic, never more so than on the Fourth of July. A great place to spend the Fourth is in any small town, but every place celebrates.
Renaissance Faire—Fairbanks, first weekend.
Golden Days—Fairbanks, third week.
Summer Arts Festival—Fairbanks, late July or early August.
World Eskimo and Indian Olympics—Fairbanks, dates vary.
Girdwood Forest Fair—Girdwood, first of month.
Halibut Derby—Homer, all month.
Homer Spit Run—Homer, fourth of July holiday.
Calamity Race—Ketchikan, first Saturday.
Timber Carnival—Ketchikan, July 4.
Tongass Pailing Race—Ketchikan, July 4.
North Pole Summer Festival—North Pole.
Bluegrass and Folk Festival—Palmer.
Horse Races—Palmer, July 4.
Mountain Marathon Race—Seward, July 4.
Silver Salmon Derby—Seward, date varies.
Soapy Smith's Wake—Skagway, July 8.
Progress Days—Soldatna, dates vary.
Moose Dropping Festival—Talkeetna, second Saturday.

AUGUST
Alaska Airmen's Association Air Show—Anchorage, date varies.
Deltana Fair—Delta Junction, first weekend.
Tanana Valley State Fair—Fairbanks, bi-annual, mid month.
Southeast Alaska State Fair—Haines, mid month.
Golden North Salmon Derby—Juneau, early in the month.
Blueberry Festival—Ketchikan, second Saturday.
Sea Test—Ketchikan, mid month.
Alaska Seafest—Ketchikan, date varies.
Kenai Peninsula State Fair—Ninilchik, dates vary.
Alaska State Fair—Palmer, date varies.
Silver Salmon Derby—Seward, date varies.
Hugs and Kisses Run—Skagway, date varies.
Eastern Star Flower Show—Skagway, mid month.

Bluegrass Festival—Talkeetna, date varies.
Gold Rush Days—Valdez, date varies.
Silver Salmon Derby—Valdez, date varies.
Silver Salmon Derby—Wrangell, date varies.

SEPTEMBER
Arts Week—Anchorage, second week.
Festival of Music—Anchorage, first two weeks.
Oktoberfest—Anchorage, mid month.
Equinox Marathon—Fairbanks, third weekend.
Perseverance Theatre—Juneau, mid month.
Klondike Trail of '98—Whitehorse, third Saturday.

INFORMATION SOURCES

For information about marine or railroad travel in Alaska:
Alaska Marine Highway System, P.O. Box 102344, Anchorage, AK 99510, Tel. 907-272-4482, Seattle: 206-623-1149; **Alaska Railroad Corporation**, P.O. Box 7-2111, Anchorage, AK 99510-7069, Tel. Anchorage: 907-265-2685 or 907-265-2494, Seattle: 206-624-4234

For information about State Parks: **State of Alaska Division of Parks and Outdoor Recreation**, 3601 C Street, 13th Floor, Anchorage, AK 99503

For information about National Forests: **U.S. Department of Agriculture, U.S. Forest Service**, Box 1268, Juneau, AK 99802; **U.S. Forest Service, Chugach National Forest**, 201 E. 9th Avenue, Anchorage, AK 99501

For information about Fish and Wildlife Refuges: **U.S. Department of the Interior, U.S. Fish and Wildlife Service**, 1011 E. Tudor Road, Anchorage, AK 99503

For information about hunting and fishing regulations: **Alaska Department of Fish and Game**, 333 Raspberry Road, Anchorage, AK 99502

For tourist information: **Alaska Division of Tourism, Department of Commerce and Economic Development**, Pouch E, Juneau, AK 99811

For information about lands administered by the Bureau of Land Management: **Bureau of Land Management** 701 C Street, Box 13, Anchorage, AK 99513

For purchase of topographic maps of Alaska: (by mail) **Alaska Distribution Unit, U.S. Geological Survey**, Box 12, Federal Bldg. (Court House), Fairbanks, AK 99701; (in person) **U.S. Geological Survey, Public Inquiries Office**, 4230 University Drive, Anchorage, AK 99508-4664

For information about mining and rock hounding: **Alaska Division of Mines and Geology**, P.O. Box 80007, College, AK 99701

For information about Native and/or Indian Affairs: **Bureau of Indian Affairs**, P.O. Box 3-8000, Juneau, AK 99802; **Bureau of Indian Affairs, Anchorage Agency**, P.O. Box 120, Anchorage, AK 99510

For Visitor Information: **Anchorage Convention and Visitors Bureau**, 201 E. Third Avenue, Anchorage, AK 99501, Tel. 907-276-4118; **Arctic Circle Chamber of Commerce**, Box 284, Kotzebue, AK 99752, Tel. 907-442-3401; **Cordova Visitors Center**, Box 1210, Cordova, AK 99574, Tel. 907-424-7443; **Fairbanks Convention and Visitors Bureau**, 550 First Avenue, Fairbanks, AK 99701, Tel. 907-766-2202; **Juneau Convention and Visitors Bureau**, 76 Egen Drive, Suite 140, Juneau, AK 99801, Tel. 907-586-1737; **Kachemak Bay Visitor and Convention Association**, Box 1001, Homer, AK 99603, Tel. 907-235-6030; **Kenai Peninsula Convention and Visitors Bureau**, Box 497, Kenai, AK 99611, Tel. 907-283-7989; **Ketchikan Visitors Bureau**, 131 Front St., Ketchikan, AK 99901, Tel. 907-225-6166; **Kodiak Island Convention and Visitors Bureau**, Box 1485, Kodiak, AK 99615, Tel. 907-486-6575; **Petersburg Visitors Information**, Box 649, Petersburg, AK 99833, Tel. 907-772-3646; **Portage Glacier Visitor Center, Anchorage District Ranger, Chugach National Forest**, Box 110469, Anchorage, AK 99511, Tel. 907-345-5700; **Seward Information Cache**, P.O. Box 756, Seward, AK 99664, Tel. 907-224-3094; **Sitka Convention and Visitors Bureau**, Box 1225, Sitka, AK 99835, Tel. 907-747-5940; **Skagway Convention and Visitors Bureau**, P.O. Box 415, Skagway, AK 99840, Tel. 907-983-2854; **Southeast Alaska Tourism Council**, Box 275, Juneau, AK 99802, Tel. 907-586-8000; **Tok Information Center**, Box 335, Tok, AK 99780, Tel. 907-883-5667; **Valdez Convention and Visitors Bureau**, P.O. Box 1603, Valdez, AK 99686, Tel. 907-835-2984; **Whittier Convention and Visitors Bureau**, 810 9th Avenue, Suite 200, Anchorage, AK 99501, Tel. 907-272-5934; **Wrangell Visitors Bureau**, Box 1078, Wrangell, AK 99929, Tel. 907-874-3770; **Yukon Visitors Bureau, Whitehorse Chamber of Commerce**, 302 Steele Street, Whitehorse, Yukon, CAN Y1A 2C5, Tel. 403-667-7545

For public transportation information: **Alaska Railroad Corporation, Passenger Services**, P.O. Box 107500, Anchorage, AK 99510-7500, Tel. Anchorage: 907-265-2685 or 907-265-2494, Seattle: 206-624-4234; **Alaska Air Lines**, P.O. Box 68900, Seattle, WA 98168, Tel. 800-426-0333; **Delta Air Lines** flies to Juneau, Anchorage and Fairbanks—Reservations: local travel agent or Tel. 800-843-9378; **Alaska Marine Highway System**, Pier 48, 101 Alaska Way South, Seattle, WA 98104, Tel. Seattle: 206-623-1149; **Admiral Cruises**, 1220 Biscayne Boulevard, Miami, FL 33101, Tel. 800-327-0271

ALASKAN WORDS AND PHRASES

Alcan   The Alaska/Canadian Highway from Dawson Creek to Fairbanks.

Aurora Borealis   The Northern Lights. Streams of light of different colors, descending from the heavens, caused by gas particles colliding with solar electrons. The results are spectacular and mystical. Best seen far north, and it must be dark for you to see them.

Bush   Any area of the outback not connected by road or ferry system.

Blue Canoes   The trusty blue vessels of the Alaska Marine Highway System.

Cache   A small storage cabin, elevated off the ground to keep food and supplies away from bears.

Cheechako   A newcomer to Alaska.

Eh   The suffix of choice in many a Canadian sentence, as in "How are you doing today, eh?"

Husky   Sled dog.

Humpie   A humpback, or pink, salmon.

Lower 48   The Alaskan term for the 48 contiguous states.

Mosquito   Alaska's unofficial "state bird".

Muskeg   A swamp or bog.

native (with a small n)   Anyone born in Alaska.

Native (with a capital N)   Denotes people of Indian or Eskimo descent.

No-see-um   Nasty little gnats of the fly family. Their bites turn into welts. Get out the long sleeves and bug juice.

Outside   Any place outside of Alaska.

Permafrost   Permanently frozen ground, covers the upper one-third of the state; scattered patches elsewhere.

Petroglyphs   Carving on rocks, often stained with mineral dyes made by the Indians.

Qiviut   The ultra-luxurious wool of the musk ox.

Sourdough   Any old timer to the state; also, the naturally occurring (and carefully husbanded) yeast to make bread and pancakes.

Taiga   This subarctic landscape of stunted trees can be seen around Mt. McKinley.

Tundra   A treeless area covered by low shrubs and mosses.

Ulu   The distinctive, fan-shaped Eskimo knife.

Williwaw   A violent gust of cold air.

PUBLICATIONS

Available at your local bookstore or directly from John Muir Publications.

22 Days Series $6.95 each, 128 to 144 pp.

These pocket-size itinerary guidebooks are a refreshing departure from ordinary guidebooks. Each author has an in-depth knowledge of the region covered and offers 22 tested daily itineraries through their favorite parts of it. Included are not only "must see" attractions but also little-known villages and hidden "jewels" as well as valuable general information.

22 Days in Alaska by Pamela Lanier (68-0) April '88
22 Days in American Southwest by Richard Harris (88-5) April '88
22 Days in Australia by John Gottberg (75-3)
22 Days in California by Roger Rapaport (93-1) Sept. '88
22 Days in China by Gaylon Duke & Zenia Victor (72-9)
22 Days in Europe by Rick Steves (62-1)
22 Days in Germany, Austria & Switzerland by Rick Steves (66-4)
22 Days in Great Britain by Rick Steves (67-2)
22 Days in Hawaii by Arnold Schuchter (92-3) Sept. '88
22 Days in India by Anurag Mathur (87-7) April '88
22 Days in Japan by David Old (73-7)
22 Days in Mexico by Steve Rogers & Tina Rosa (64-8)
22 Days in New England by Arnold Schuchter (96-6) Sept. '88
22 Days in New Zealand by Arnold Schuchter (86-9) April '88
22 Days in Norway, Denmark & Sweden by Rick Steves (83-4)
22 Days in Pacific Northwest by Richard Harris (97-4) Oct. '88
22 Days in Spain & Portugal by Rick Steves (63-X)
22 Days in West Indies by Cyndy & Sam Morreale (74-5)

Undiscovered Islands of the Caribbean, Burl Willis $12.95   (80-X)   220 pp.

For the past decade, Burl Willis has been tracking down remote Caribbean getaways—the kind known only to the most adventurous traveler. Here he offers complete information on 32 islands—all you'll need to know for a vacation in an as yet undiscovered Paradise.

People's Guide to Mexico, Carl Franz
$13.95   (56-7)   560 pp.

Now in its 12th printing, this classic guide shows the traveler how to handle just about any situation that might arise while in Mexico. "...the best 360-degree coverage of traveling and short-term living in Mexico that's going."—
Whole Earth Epilog.

People's Guide to RV Camping in Mexico, Carl Franz $12.95 (91-5) 356 pp.

The sequel to *The People's Guide to Mexico,* this revised guide focuses on the special pleasures and challenges of RV travel in Mexico. An unprecedented number of Americans and Canadians have discovered the advantages of RV travel in reaching remote villages and camping comfortably on beaches. Sept '88

The On and Off the Road Cookbook, Carl Franz $8.50 (27-3) 272 pp.

Carl Franz, (*The People's Guide to Mexico)* and Lorena Havens offer a multitude of delicious alternatives to the usual campsite meals or roadside cheeseburgers. Over 120 proven recipes.

The Shopper's Guide to Mexico, Steve Rogers & Tina Rosa $9.95 (90-7) 200 pp.

The only comprehensive handbook for shopping in Mexico, this guide ferrets out little-known towns where the finest handicrafts are made and offers shopping techniques for judging quality, bargaining, and complete information on packaging, mailing and U.S. customs requirements. Sept '88

The Heart of Jerusalem, Arlynn Nellhaus $12.95 (79-6) 312 pp.

Denver Post journalist Arlynn Nellhaus draws on her vast experience in and knowledge of Jerusalem to give travelers a rare inside view and practical guide to the Golden City—from holy sites and religious observances to how to shop for toothpaste and use the telephone.

Guide to Buddhist Meditation Retreats, Don Morreale $12.95 (94-X) 312 pp.

The only comprehensive directory of Buddhist centers, this guide includes first-person narratives of individuals' retreat experiences. Invaluable for both newcomers and experienced practitioners who wish to expand their contacts within the American Buddhist Community. Sept. '88

Complete Guide to Bed & Breakfasts, Inns & Guesthouses, Pamela Lanier $13.95 (82-6) 520 pp.

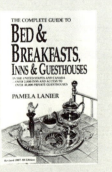

Newly revised and the most complete directory, with over 4800 listings in all 50 states, 10 Canadian provinces, Puerto Rico and the U.S. Virgin Islands. This classic provides details on reservation services and indexes identifying inns noted for antiques, decor, conference facilities and gourmet food.

All-Suite Hotel Guide, Pamela Lanier $11.95 (70-2) 312 pp.

Pamela Lanier, author of *The Complete Guide to Bed & Breakfasts, Inns & Guesthouses,* now provides the discerning traveler with a listing of over 600 all-suite hotels. Indispensable for families traveling with children or business people requiring an extra meeting room.

Elegant Small Hotels, Pamela Lanier $13.95 (77-X) 202 pp.

This lodging guide for discriminating travelers describes 168 American hotels characterized by exquisite rooms and suites and personal service par excellence. Includes small hotels in 35 states and the Caribbean with many photos in full color.

Gypsying After 40, Bob Harris $12.95 (71-0) 312 pp.

Retirees Bob and Megan Harris offer a witty and informative guide to the "gypsying" lifestyle that has enriched their lives and can enrich yours. For 10 of the last 18 years they have traveled throughout the world living out of camper vans and boats. Their message is: "Anyone can do it'!!

Mona Winks, A Guide to Enjoying the Museum of Europe, Rick Steves $12.95 (85-0) 356 pp.

Here's a guide that will save you time, shoe leather and tired muscles. It's designed for people who want to get the most out of visiting the great museums of Europe. It covers 25 museums in London, Paris, Rome, Venice, Florence, Amsterdam, Munich, Madrid and Vienna.

Europe Through The Back Door, Rick Steves $12.95 (84-2) 404 pp.

Doubleday and Literary Guild Bookclub Selection.

For people who want to enjoy Europe more and spend less money doing it. In this revised edition, Rick shares more of his well-respected insights. He also describes his favorite "back doors"—less visited destinations throughout Europe that are a wonderful addition to any European vacation.

Europe 101, Rick Steves & Gene Openshaw $11.95 (78-8) 372 pp.

The first and only jaunty history and art book for travelers makes castles, palaces and museums come alive. Both Steves and Openshaw hold degrees in European history, but their real education has come from escorting first-time visitors throughout Europe.

Asia Through The Back Door, Rick Steves & John Gottberg $11.95 (58-3) 336 pp.

In this detailed guide book are information and advice you won't find elsewhere—including how to overcome culture shock, bargain in marketplaces, observe Buddhist temple etiquette and, possibly most important of all, how to eat noodles with chopsticks!

Traveler's Guide to Asian Culture, John Gottberg $12.95 (81-8) 356 pp.

John Gottberg, *Insight Guide* editor and co-author with Rick Steves of *Asia Through the Back Door,* has written for the traveler an accurate and enjoyable guide to the history and culture of this diverse continent. Sept. '88

Guide to Bus Touring in the U.S., Stuart Warren & Douglas Block $11.95 (95-8) 256 pp.

For many people, bus touring is the ideal, relaxed and comfortable way to see America. The author has had years of experience as a bus tour conductor and writes in-depth about every aspect of bus touring to help passengers get the most pleasure for their money. Sept. '88

Road & Track's Used Car Classics edited by Peter Bohr $12.95 (69-9) 272 pp.

Road & Track contributing editor Peter Bohr has compiled this collection of the magazine's "Used Car Classic" articles, updating them to include current market information. Over 70 makes and models of American, British, Italian, West German, Swedish and Japanese enthusiast cars built between 1953 and 1979 are featured.

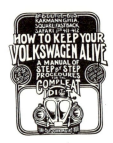

Automotive Repair Manuals

Each JMP automotive manual gives clear step-by-step instructions, together with illustrations that show exactly how each system in the vehicle comes apart and goes back together. They tell everything a novice or experienced mechanic needs to know to perform periodic maintenance, tune-ups, troubleshooting and repair of the brake, fuel and emission control, electrical, cooling, clutch, transmission, driveline, steering and suspension systems, and even rebuild the engine.

How To Keep Your VW Alive $17.95 (50-8) 384 pp.
How To Keep Your VW Rabbit Alive $17.95 (47-8) 440 pp.
How To Keep Your Honda Car Alive $17.95 (55-9) 272 pp.
How To Keep Your Subaru Alive $17.95 (49-4) 464 pp.
How To Keep Your Toyota Pick-Up Alive $17.95 (89-3) 400 pp. April '88
How To Keep Your Datsun/Nissan Alive $22.95 (65-6) 544 pp.
How To Keep Your Honda ATC Alive $14.95 (45-1) 236 pp.

ITEM NO.			TITLE	EACH	QUAN.	TOTAL
		·				
		·				
		·				
		·				
		·				
		·				

Subtotals _____

Postage & handling (see ordering information)* _____

New Mexicans please add 5.625% tax _____

Total Amount Due _____

METHOD OF PAYMENT (circle one)   MC   VISA   AMEX   CHECK   MONEY ORDER

Credit Card Number   Expiration Date

Signature X _____
Required for Credit Card Purchases

Telephone: Office (____) _____ Home (____) _____

Name _____

Address _____

City _____ State _____ Zip _____

See reverse side for Ordering Information

ORDERING INFORMATION

Fill in the order blank. Be sure to add up all of the subtotals at the bottom of the order form, and give us the address whither your order will be whisked.

Postage & Handling

Your books will be sent to you via UPS (for U.S. destinations), and you will receive them in approximately 10 days from the time that we receive your order.

Include $2.75 for the first item ordered and add $.50 for each additional item to cover shipping and handling costs. UPS shipments to post office boxes take longer to arrive; if possible, please give us a street address.

For airmail within the U.S., enclose $4.00 per book for shipping and handling.

ALL FOREIGN ORDERS will be shipped surface rate. Please enclose $3.00 for the first item and $1.00 for each additional item. Please inquire for airmail rates.

Method of Payment

Your order may be paid by check, money order or credit card. We cannot be responsible for cash sent through the mail.

All payments must be in U.S. dollars drawn on a U.S. bank. Canadian postal money orders in U.S. dollars also accepted.

For VISA, Mastercard or American Express orders, use the order form or call (505) 982-4078. Books ordered on American Express cards can be shipped only to the billing address of the cardholder.

Sorry, no C.O.D.'s.

Residents of sunny New Mexico add 5.625% to the total.

Backorders

We will backorder all forthcoming and out-of-stock titles unless otherwise requested.

Address all orders and inquiries to:

JOHN MUIR PUBLICATIONS
P.O. Box 613
Santa Fe, NM 87504
(505) 982-4078

All prices subject to change without notice.